The Journey Begins

Other titles by Avril Rowlands

All the Tales From the Ark

The Animals' Caravan

The Journey Begins

Adventures through the Bible
with Caravan Bear and friends

Woodlands C of E Primary School

Avril Rowlands

Illustrated by Kay Widdowson

LION
CHILDREN'S

To Marilyn, with love and thanks for
Christopher Rabbit

Text copyright © 2018 Avril Rowlands
Illustrations copyright © 2018 Kay Widdowson
This edition copyright © 2018 Lion Hudson IP Limited

The right of Avril Rowlands to be identified as the author and of Kay Widdowson to be identified as the illustrator of this work has been asserted by them in accordance with the Copyright, Designs and Patents Act 1988.

All rights reserved. No part of this publication may be reproduced or transmitted in any form or by any means, electronic or mechanical, including photocopy, recording, or any information storage and retrieval system, without permission in writing from the publisher.

Published by Lion Children's Books
an imprint of
Lion Hudson Limited
Wilkinson House, Jordan Hill Business Park,
Banbury Road, Oxford OX2 8DR, England
www.lionhudson.com/lionchildrens

ISBN 978 0 7459 7756 0

First edition 2018

A catalogue record for this book is available from the British Library

Printed and bound in the UK, March 2018, LH26

Contents

1 The Caravan Sets Off   7
2 Adam and Eve *Genesis 2-3*   18
3 The Two Brothers *Genesis 4*   32
4 Jonah's Watery Adventure *Jonah*   42
5 The Babbling Tower *Genesis 11*   59
6 Noah and the Flood *Genesis 6-9*   72
7 Joseph and His Brothers *Genesis 37*   85
8 Crossing the Red Sea *Exodus 4-14*   100
9 Ruth's New Home *Ruth*   120

The Caravan Sets Off

It was spring, and Hector the horse sniffed the warm, sweet air. The sun shone on his back, birds were busy calling to each other as they built their nests, and the trees that fringed the paddock were beginning to unfurl bright green leaves. Everything around him was fresh and new.

Hector took to his heels. "It's time to be off!" he shouted as he raced round and round the field. "Time we were off on our travels!"

In the small garden beside the paddock, Whitby the dog waved her tail. She also felt excited. "Wake up, Caravan Bear! It's spring."

"I'm not asleep," Caravan Bear said as he left his house and crossed the garden. He was carrying a paintbrush and a can of bright red paint. "I've been up for hours, painting the caravan so that it looks smart for our journey."

"I don't know about painting the caravan," said Whitby. "You seem to have painted yourself!" It was true. Caravan Bear was covered in red and yellow paint.

"Oh dear! Never mind. I've almost finished. Then I've just got to stock up with food for our journey, and we'll be off."

"Where are we going?" asked Whitby.

"Anywhere and everywhere," said Caravan Bear.

Just a few months ago, he thought, he did not own a caravan at all. He didn't own a horse either. Last autumn he and his dog Whitby were out for a walk and spotted what looked like a broken-down van backed into a hedge in the corner of a farmer's field. Whitby raced over to have a closer look and Caravan Bear followed.

Not, he thought, that he was known then as Caravan Bear. That came later. At the time everyone just called him Bear.

When he got nearer, he saw the remains of a gypsy-style caravan. It had once been painted red with yellow wheels but much of the paint had worn away and the bare wood showed through. It was surrounded by weeds and long grass and looked as if it had been there for a long, long time.

Caravan Bear tried to peer inside but the doorway was too high up.

"Here's some steps!" called Whitby, who was searching around in the hedge. Between them they dragged the three steps over to the caravan, clipped them on to the front, climbed up, and peered inside. They saw a big bed at one end, a dresser running the length of one wall, and more cupboards and a stove on the other. The remains of a chair lay on its side. As they watched, a family of mice ran across the floor and out through a hole in the side.

"Oh," said Caravan Bear. "It's lovely."

"No, it's not," Whitby retorted. "It's all broken and filthy and the rain's got in through that hole." She sniffed. "And it's very smelly."

"So would you be if you'd been living outside in the corner of a farmer's field for goodness knows how long."

Caravan Bear climbed inside. "It could be made beautiful," he said. He could picture it mended with shiny polished wood, cups and saucers and plates on hooks on the dresser, a table and chair with a soft cushion, lamps giving a warm glow, and a brightly coloured rug on the floor. "I could mend it and paint it and we could go travelling in it all spring and summer."

"Why?"

"Why not? We could go and see places we've never seen and have all sorts of adventures!"

Whitby barked loudly. It sounded a good idea to her.

Caravan Bear smiled as he remembered going to find the farmer to ask if he could buy the caravan.

"That old thing?" the farmer said. "If you take it away, you can have it for nothing."

"Oh, thank you!"

"I was about to chop it up for firewood."

"You mustn't do that!" Caravan Bear was shocked.

"How are you going to move it?" asked the farmer.

Caravan Bear scratched his head.

"I don't know. I haven't thought…"

"Well," said the farmer, a rather sly look coming into his eyes. "If you'd like to buy my old horse over there…"

Caravan Bear looked over to where a horse was

standing in a muddy patch of the field beside a gate. It was a dirty and sad-looking horse, and so thin that Caravan Bear could see his ribs sticking out under his skin.

"Um…"

"You'll need a horse to tow the caravan," the farmer added. "And that one's good for towing, if not for much else."

"He doesn't look very strong…"

"Oh, he is," the farmer assured him. "Hector's his name."

Hector the horse looked up and Caravan Bear was shocked to see the unhappy look on his face.

"All right," he said, and paid the farmer a large amount of money for a horse that looked as if it wouldn't be strong enough to tow anything. But Hector was stronger than he looked. Happy to be leaving the farmer, he quickly pulled the caravan out of the field, along the road, and down to the village that was home to Caravan Bear and Whitby.

"We'll have to call you Caravan Bear now!" Whitby shouted, running alongside the van. And the name stuck.

All winter long Caravan Bear worked hard. First

he made a shelter and paddock for Hector in the field beside his house. He fed him lots of fresh oats until his ribs stopped showing and his coat gleamed. Then he hammered and sawed and cleaned and painted until the caravan shone brightly in the spring sunshine.

"Come on!" said Whitby. "We haven't all day!"

"Oh yes, we have," said Caravan Bear. "We've all spring and all summer."

He smiled happily.

That same day, in a house in the next village, Christopher Rabbit also sniffed the air when he woke up. It felt... different. Of course! He bounded out of bed. It was his birthday! He smiled – but a moment later he stopped smiling. It was his birthday, but no one had given him any presents. He hadn't even had any cards.

"Perhaps it's my own fault," he thought. "I don't really know many animals – so why should anyone know it's my birthday? It's very sad, but I don't think I have any friends. Not real ones. I don't know where you find them."

Christopher Rabbit was quite a shy rabbit, but a

few days earlier he had sent out some invitation cards to the animals living around him, inviting them to a party to celebrate his birthday. He had stocked up with lots of food.

But no one had come.

Christopher Rabbit sighed, sat down at the kitchen table, and ate the party food himself – or as much as he could. When he had finished eating – and was feeling very full indeed – he came to a decision.

"It's no good sitting here being miserable," he said out loud. "I must go and make some friends."

He put on his scarf, went outside, walked up the garden path… and fell right over a parcel sitting in the road.

The parcel was wrapped in shiny golden paper, tied up with silver string. There was a label attached that waved in the breeze. "CHRISTOPHER RABBIT" was handwritten on it in large letters.

Christopher Rabbit stared at it.

It was a present. Someone had sent him a present!

Forgetting that he was sitting in the middle of the road (which was a dangerous place to sit), he tore open the wrapping. Inside was a book with the words "THE BIBLE" on the cover. He opened the book.

On the first page inside, he read "Read Me" in the same handwriting.

"How very odd," he thought.

Just then, another odd thing happened.

"Clip clop, clip clop!"

A horse was racing down the centre of the road, straight toward him. It was pulling a brightly painted caravan with red body and yellow wheels, which was swaying from side to side. Holding tightly on the top step was a small bear and an even smaller dog.

"Out of my way!" shouted the horse.

Christopher Rabbit stood up and put up his hand.

"Stop!" he shouted. He closed his eyes and waited for the crash.

The horse stopped a whisker's length from his face.

"What did you do that for?" Hector asked angrily. "I was enjoying myself."

Caravan Bear climbed down shakily. "Thank you," he said to Christopher Rabbit. "If Hector had gone much faster, he would have overturned the caravan."

"That's all right," said Christopher Rabbit. "It's the second odd thing that's happened today."

"What was the first one?" asked Whitby.

"It was a book," said Christopher Rabbit, "lying in the road, addressed to me. I fell over it."

"What was it doing lying in the road?" asked Hector.

"I don't know."

"Who sent it?" asked Whitby.

"I don't know that either," said Christopher Rabbit. "It's my birthday, you see, and it's the only present I've had."

"That solves it," said Caravan Bear. "It's a birthday present."

"Yes, but I don't know who sent it so I can't say thank you."

"Isn't there anything written in it?" asked Hector.

"Just 'Read me'," said Christopher Rabbit.

The animals thought for a moment.

"Perhaps God sent it," said Caravan Bear.

"Why would he do that?" asked Christopher Rabbit.

The bear shrugged. "Perhaps he wants you to read it?"

Christopher Rabbit turned the pages and began to read. He was soon so interested that he forgot all about the caravan.

"It's got lots of good stories in it," he said.

Hector snorted. "It's a bit boring standing in the

middle of the road while you read your book," he said. "Why don't you move it and yourself out of the way so we can get on with our journey?"

Christopher Rabbit looked up. "Where are you going?" he asked.

"Oh, here…" began Caravan Bear.

"And there…" said Whitby eagerly.

"Wherever the fancy takes us," added Hector.

Christopher Rabbit thought for a moment. "I've never been to 'here' or 'there'," he said slowly. "Or 'wherever the fancy takes us'." He thought they all sounded interesting places.

"Let's take him on board – then he can read his book while we travel, and tell us the stories when we stop," said Hector, impatient to be off.

"Are you sure?" asked Christopher Rabbit shyly. "I don't want to be a nuisance or anything…"

"Come on," said Whitby. "We haven't all day!"

"Do come," said Caravan Bear. "We'd love to have you."

So Christopher Rabbit lifted the book from the road and carried it up the steps into the caravan.

He had found some friends.

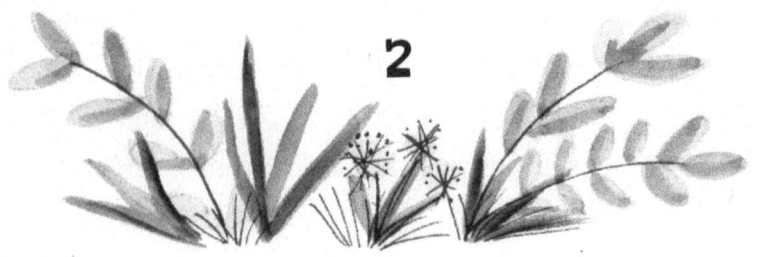

2

Adam and Eve

"Travel slowly, Hector," said Caravan Bear. "We've had enough excitement for one day."

Hector snorted and set off at full speed.

While they journeyed through the countryside, Caravan Bear watched the road ahead and Whitby looked at the passing scenery, but Christopher Rabbit kept his nose firmly inside his new book.

When the sun began to set, Hector turned off the road. He stopped in a field under the shade of a large tree.

Christopher Rabbit looked up. "Why have we stopped?" he asked.

"I'm tired," said Hector.

"And I'm hungry," said Caravan Bear.

ADAM AND EVE

"It'll be dark soon – and I'm scared of the dark," said Whitby.

They had their supper, and then Caravan Bear lit the lamps inside the caravan. They all sat down, apart from Hector – who put his nose in through the open window.

"Now tell us a story," said Caravan Bear.

"Where shall I start?" asked Christopher Rabbit.

"Why not at the beginning?" said Caravan Bear, and they all agreed that it was a good place to start.

THE JOURNEY BEGINS

"The first story in the book is about a garden," Christopher Rabbit began.

"Rather like this one," said Whitby.

Christopher Rabbit looked through the window. "No, not like this one," he said. "This is a field, not a garden. It's a very nice field, but the garden in the story was wonderful. It was made by God and it was full of every sort of flower and every sort of tree, and the grass was green and thick. It was called the Garden of Eden."

"Were there any dogs in the garden?" asked Whitby.

"Dogs aren't in the story," replied Christopher Rabbit, "but that doesn't mean there weren't any."

"What about horses?" asked Hector.

"They're not in the story either."

"Bears?" asked Caravan Bear.

Christopher Rabbit shook his head. "I don't even know if there were any rabbits."

"Bit of a dull story, then," said Hector.

"No, it's not," said Christopher Rabbit. He thought they might throw him out of the caravan if they didn't like the story – and he didn't know where he was. He didn't like the dark, either.

He went on quickly. "In the middle of the garden, God planted two trees. One was the Tree of Life and the other the Tree of the Knowledge of Good and Evil."

"Funny names," said Whitby.

"Why give them such complicated names?" asked Hector. "Why not just call them simple names like 'oak' or 'ash'?"

"I don't know," said Christopher Rabbit. He went on. "After God had made the garden he made human beings. He made the first man and named him Adam and he made the first woman and named her Eve."

"I don't like the name Adam," said Hector. "I prefer Hector."

"God didn't ask you," said Whitby.

"Adam and Eve looked at themselves. They looked at their arms and they looked at their legs. They liked what they saw. They took deep breaths of air. They liked what they felt. They looked around and saw the beautiful garden God had made.

"'It's all yours,' God told them. 'Oh, just one thing. You can go anywhere and eat anything apart from the fruit from that tree over there.'"

"Why?" asked Whitby. "Was it poisonous?"

THE JOURNEY BEGINS

"Probably, because God said that if they ate the fruit from that tree they would die," said Christopher Rabbit. "'Thank you,' said Adam and Eve, and they wandered off. God watched them go and thought they looked a bit lonely by themselves."

"Poor Adam," said Hector, sniffing.

"Poor Eve," added Whitby.

"So God brought every animal and every bird to Adam and Eve so that they could name them."

"Like Hector?" asked Hector.

ADAM AND EVE

"No – like 'horse'," said Christopher Rabbit.

"We've already found out that horses don't appear in this story," Whitby pointed out.

"So how did I get my name?" asked Hector.

No-one answered.

"Why did God want to make humans anyway?" Whitby wondered.

"I don't know," said Christopher Rabbit.

"And why did he want them in his garden?" Whitby

went on. "It would probably have gone along very nicely with just the animals, insects, and birds."

"And fish," added Caravan Bear.

"There aren't any fish in a garden," said Hector. "Unless there was a pond there."

Christopher Rabbit considered this. "I expect God wanted Adam and Eve to look after the garden when he wasn't around."

"They probably had a vegetable patch," said Hector wisely. Before he belonged to the farmer he used to work in a market garden and knew all about vegetables.

"In the evening, God would come and talk to Adam and Eve."

"What did they talk about?" asked Whitby.

"Oh, I imagine it was what they'd been doing that day and the state of the weather and things like that," said Christopher Rabbit vaguely.

"What had God been doing all day?" asked Caravan Bear. "Gardening?"

"The story doesn't say, but I expect God was having a rest as he'd just spent six days creating the world – so he must have been very tired," Christopher Rabbit replied.

They all agreed that God deserved a rest after creating the world.

"Adam and Eve lived in the garden and were very happy until Eve met the snake."

"You never mentioned a snake!" cried Caravan Bear.

"I was saving it," said Christopher Rabbit. "I said the story got exciting."

"I don't like snakes," said Whitby with a shiver. "Not that I've ever seen one – just heard about them."

"Why is a snake mentioned in the story, but no dog, horse, or bear?" demanded Hector.

"I don't know. I didn't write it," sighed Christopher Rabbit. "There's no rabbit, either, but I'm not complaining. Do you want me to go on or not?"

The other three agreed that he should go on.

"The snake was very clever," Christopher Rabbit continued, "and very cunning. 'Look,' he said to Eve. 'You won't die if you eat the fruit from the Tree of Knowledge of Good and Evil. All that stuff God told you about it was just to put you off.

"'You could be as wise and clever as God,' the snake hissed, 'if you eat the fruit.'

"Eve looked at the fruit hanging from the tree.

It looked lovely and tasty.

"She thought how wonderful it would be to be as wise and clever as God.

"Day after day the snake followed Eve until at last she gave in. She picked one of the fruit, ate some of it, and gave the rest to Adam."

"Was it an apple?" asked Whitby.

"It doesn't say what fruit it was in the story," Christopher Rabbit replied.

Caravan Bear stood up. "All this talk of food is making me hungry," he said. "Anyone for cheese and biscuits?"

As they munched their cheese and biscuits, Whitby suddenly asked, "I don't understand – why did the snake want Eve to eat the fruit?"

"Perhaps he just wanted to spoil things," said

Hector, through a mouthful of oats. He had not wanted cheese and biscuits. "Some animals are like that. They just want to spoil things for others."

"Perhaps the snake was jealous of Adam and Eve," said Christopher Rabbit.

"Might have been," said Whitby. "I don't expect God stopped to chat to the snake in the evening – do you?"

Caravan Bear was eating his cheese and biscuits slowly, thinking hard. "If God made everything in the world, why did he make something as nasty as the snake?" he asked.

"Or spiders," said Whitby. "I don't like spiders."

Christopher Rabbit thought about it, then shook his head. "I don't know, but I expect he had his reasons," he added.

"Well, I think it was a bit awful of God to put this lovely fruit in the garden and then tell Adam and Eve they mustn't eat it," said Whitby, taking the last biscuit.

"Why?" asked Hector.

"It's just inviting them to do something they shouldn't," said Whitby, grabbing the last piece of cheese as well.

"I don't think it's awful," said Caravan Bear. "It was God's garden. Why shouldn't he make rules for those who lived in it? It's my caravan and I have rules."

"I didn't know you had any rules," mumbled Whitby, her mouth full.

"Well, I do," said Caravan Bear firmly. "One rule is not being greedy and grabbing the last biscuit and cheese for yourself. You should have offered it to our guest."

"Sorry," said Whitby.

"Another rule is clearing up after your mess," said Caravan Bear, looking at the pile of crumbs on the floor around Whitby.

There was a pause while Whitby cleared up the crumbs. Then Hector asked, "What happened next?"

"God arrived," said Christopher Rabbit.

"Trouble," said Whitby, shaking her head.

"Big trouble," agreed Caravan Bear.

"What did Adam and Eve do?" asked Hector.

"They hid," said Christopher Rabbit, "because they realized that they hadn't obeyed God."

"I don't blame them," said Whitby. "I'd have hidden too."

"Did God beat them?" asked Hector. "The farmer

used to beat me, but he stopped after I kicked him."

"God doesn't beat anyone up," said Christopher Rabbit. "That's not his way."

"Oh," said Hector, slightly disappointed.

"When he found them, God asked, 'Why did you eat the fruit from that tree?'

"'It wasn't my fault,' Adam said. 'It was her. She made me.'

"'It wasn't my fault, either,' Eve said. 'It was the snake. He tricked me.'"

"I hope God did something about that snake," said Hector. "He sounds nasty."

"I'm not really sure that it was *all* the snake's fault," said Christopher Rabbit, thinking about it. "Eve could have said no. So could Adam. It's very easy to blame others for things."

"I'm always being blamed," said Hector.

"What for?" asked Christopher Rabbit.

"Everything," said Hector gloomily.

"Now that's not true," said Caravan Bear. "But often it *is* your fault."

"What is?" asked Christopher Rabbit.

"Everything," said Caravan Bear.

"So what *did* God do if he didn't beat them up?"

asked Whitby, anxious to hear the rest of the story.

"God was very sad. He had given Adam and Eve this lovely garden and all the delicious food in it — and they'd spoiled it. He told them they would have to leave the garden where they'd been so happy, and he sent an angel with a sword to guard the way to the Tree of Life."

"That was a bit hard," said Caravan Bear.

"Well," said Christopher Rabbit, "they did break God's rules. But he also told them that he would always be there if they wanted him."

He closed the book.

"What happened next?" demanded Whitby.

"That's another story," Christopher Rabbit replied.

"And it's late and I'm tired," said Caravan Bear. "I think we should go to bed."

But before Christopher Rabbit went to bed, he left the caravan and walked into the field.

The branches of the tree waved in a gentle breeze over his head. Above them arched the black sky, which was studded with white stars.

"Thank you, God, for giving me these friends," he said. "And thank you for sending me the book of your stories."

ADAM AND EVE

He was suddenly very tired and started to climb the steps into the caravan. He heard a rustle – and then something hard hit him on the head and went bouncing down the steps to lie in the grass.

Christopher Rabbit bent down and picked it up. It was a small, wizened apple, the last one to fall from the tree.

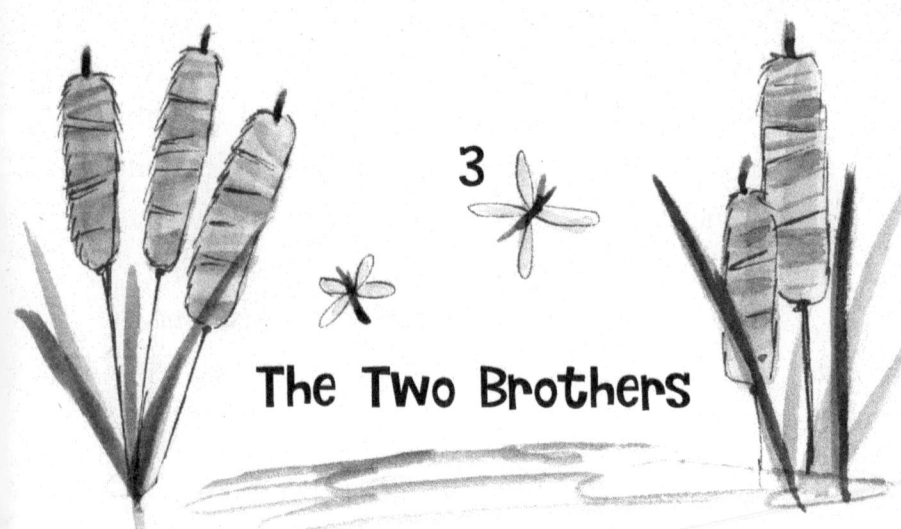

The Two Brothers

"Whatever is that noise?" Whitby complained, poking her head out of the window of the caravan. They had parked in a field beside a large pond.

"It's two geese," said Caravan Bear, coming up the caravan steps. "I think they're fighting."

A duck waddled over. "It's Gracie and George," she said gloomily. "Brother and sister. George is a bully – always getting at Gracie. I'll be glad when they push off back to wherever they came from."

"*I'm* leading the flock on our journey!" shouted one of the geese. It was George.

"No, I am," Gracie said quietly. "The flock asked me to."

"They're stupid, then!" George shouted back.

He flew up from the pond and began hissing.

Then he flapped his wings, circled around, and began pecking at Gracie, tearing out her feathers.

"Stop that!" shouted Caravan Bear.

"I'm older," George shouted back, flapping his wings again, "so I'm leading our flock north for the summer. She's just jealous, 'cos she's not in charge!"

"You're the one who's jealous," said Gracie.

George flew at her again, pecking, squawking, and flapping his wings.

"If he tears any more feathers off that poor bird, there'll be enough to stuff a cushion," said Whitby hopefully. "I could do with a nice goose feather cushion to sleep on."

Christopher Rabbit stuck his head around the caravan door. "If you stop fighting, I'll tell you a story from the Bible," he said.

"It had better be a short one," said George importantly. "The wind's changing so we haven't much time before we set off."

"It's a sad story," said Christopher Rabbit, "about two brothers."

"I'd rather have a happy story about two sisters," said Gracie.

"Their names were Cain and Abel," Christopher Rabbit continued. "They lived on a farm and their parents were Adam and Eve."

"You've already told us that story," said Hector.

Christopher Rabbit ignored him and carried on. "Cain was older than Abel. When they grew up, Cain grew the crops on the farm while Abel looked after the animals.

"Although they were brothers, they were very different. Cain was a jealous sort of person, who got angry very quickly and liked picking quarrels. Abel seems to have been quieter and gentler than his brother. He went out of his way to avoid trouble."

"I'm like Abel," said Gracie firmly. "It's George who picks all the quarrels."

"You've got to be joking!" cried George.

The two geese glared at each other.

Christopher Rabbit settled himself with his book on the caravan steps. "In the autumn, at harvest time, both sons gave presents to God."

"Why did they give God presents?" asked Caravan Bear.

"Perhaps they were trying to bribe God," Hector suggested. "You know, like the time you promised me extra oats if I would pull the caravan a bit further."

"That's different," Caravan Bear protested.

"I don't think you can bribe God," said Christopher Rabbit. "And I don't think the presents were meant as bribes. I think they were just meant as 'thank you' for a good harvest and good and healthy sheep. Cain gave some of his crops, while Abel brought God one of his best lambs."

"I like being given presents," Whitby smiled and added wistfully, "I would really like a present of a nice feather-filled cushion."

"You shouldn't ask for presents," said Caravan Bear. "Then you won't be disappointed when you don't get them."

"Oh, get on with the story," said George impatiently.

Christopher Rabbit turned the page of his book. "Cain knew, deep down, that God wasn't pleased with him. This might have been because Abel gave God the best he had, but Cain gave God some crops that weren't very good."

"You mean like the spindly ones that no one would want to eat?" asked Hector.

"Possibly."

"Why did that matter to God?" Hector asked.

"I think because it showed that Cain didn't really think that God was important enough to have the best. Anyway, Cain thought that God preferred his brother to him, and he probably thought that that wasn't fair."

"Life isn't always fair," said Hector sadly.

"So *did* God prefer Abel?" asked Whitby.

"I don't think God takes sides," Christopher Rabbit replied. "He might not have been pleased with Cain and felt his second-rate offering was a bit sad, but I expect he loved Cain and cared about him just as much as he cared about his brother.

"But Cain didn't believe that. He just grew more and more jealous of Abel."

"'I'll get even with him,' Cain thought as he watched Abel lead his sheep out to the fields."

"What was God doing in all this?" asked Whitby.

"He should have told him off," said Hector.

"He did," replied Christopher Rabbit, "but Cain

took no notice. Soon he hated his brother so much that he couldn't think of anything else."

Christopher Rabbit stopped.

"Go on!" cried Gracie.

"Don't stop there," urged George, for once agreeing with his sister.

Christopher Rabbit gave them both a look, and then went back to his book. "One dreadful day Cain asked Abel to go for a walk with him. They went out into the country. When they were out of sight of the village, Cain turned on Abel and killed him."

"Dead?" squeaked Whitby.

"Dead," said Christopher Rabbit.

"That's really awful," said Whitby. "I don't like this story."

"I said it was sad," Christopher Rabbit reminded them. "Not all the stories in the Bible are happy."

"They're good stories though," Caravan Bear replied.

"I like a bit of blood," said Hector.

"Oh, come on," Caravan Bear laughed. "Who burst into tears when he cut his knee on a bramble?"

"That was different," Hector insisted. "It hurt a lot."

THE TWO BROTHERS

"What happened to Cain?" asked Gracie quietly.

Christopher Rabbit looked down at his book. "God spoke to him. He asked him where his brother was."

"Why did God do that?" asked Whitby. "I mean, Abel was lying there dead, so God couldn't have missed seeing him."

"I expect he wanted to see if Cain would be honest with him," Caravan Bear remarked.

"And was he?" asked George, also in quite a quiet voice.

"No," said Christopher Rabbit. "He just shouted, 'How should I know? I'm not my brother's keeper!'"

"You shouldn't speak to God like that," said Caravan Bear.

"You shouldn't kill your brother, either," Hector added.

"What did God do?" asked Gracie.

"Strike him dead?" suggested George.

"No," said Christopher Rabbit. "He sent Cain away from his home and his family for ever. And he put a sign on Cain's forehead to make sure no one tried to kill him for what he'd done."

"Why?" asked Gracie.

"Perhaps God wanted to forgive him and give him another chance. Perhaps he thought that everyone's life is important, even Cain's.

"Perhaps he felt that he'd be some sort of warning to everyone who met him that people shouldn't be jealous or fight with their family." Christopher Rabbit shut his book.

There was a silence.

"I don't mind if you lead the other geese when we leave," Gracie muttered to George.

"No, you'd be better," said George. "The flock asked you."

Together they went back to the pond.

"Oh dear," said the duck. "I hope they don't start fighting again."

"So do I," agreed Christopher Rabbit, watching them go.

He felt rather sad inside because he didn't have any brothers or sisters, even if, like George and Gracie, they fought a lot. That evening he went off by himself for a walk.

Suddenly he heard a loud whooshing of wings, and the air was filled with the cries of geese. He looked up to see the entire flock rise from the pond, circle, and turn away toward the north, fanned out behind one goose – the leader.

Christopher Rabbit held his paw up to his eyes but couldn't see whether the leader was Gracie or George as they were flying too fast and too high.

The sounds died away and Christopher Rabbit looked back at the caravan. The lights had been lit and shone with a warm and friendly glow. He smiled.

"At least I've some good friends now," he thought. "Thank you, God."

And he made his way back to the caravan and a welcome meal.

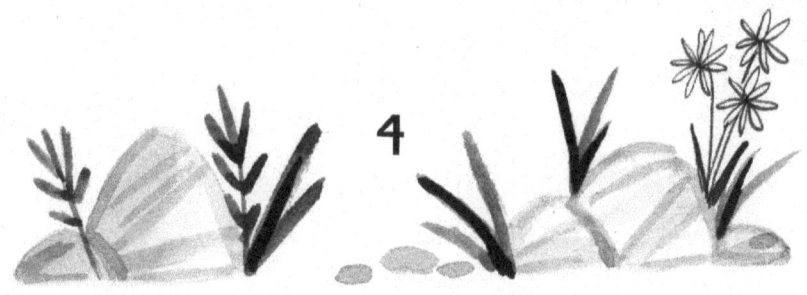

Jonah's Watery Adventure

"I'm bored," said Whitby. She was sitting on the riverbank watching Caravan Bear fishing.

"So am I," said Hector, pulling at a clump of grass. "We've been here for ages and I'm hot."

"I'm hot and I'm hungry," Whitby added. "It's all right for you, Hector – you can eat grass."

Hector turned up his nose. "It's not very nice grass."

Whitby sighed. "At least it's food. Caravan Bear hasn't caught anything and I was looking forward to fish and chips for supper."

Caravan Bear glanced around. "Won't be a minute," he said. "I'm sure there's a nice big fish out there."

Christopher Rabbit, who had been reading his book, looked up at them. "Shall I tell you a story

while we're waiting for Caravan Bear to catch a fish?" he asked.

"Oh yes," said Caravan Bear.

"Is there a story about a fish in your book?" asked Whitby.

"There are all kinds of stories," said Christopher Rabbit. "But here's a really good fishy one."

He turned the page and began.

"This story is about a man called Jonah. He was an ordinary kind of man who probably liked a quiet life."

"Don't we all?" remarked Hector, who had stopped eating.

"One day, God asked him to go to a city called

Nineveh and tell the people there to mend their ways. God said that the people had grown wicked and evil. If they didn't change, he – God, that is – would destroy the city and everyone in it, forty days after Jonah had delivered his message."

"Why didn't God tell the people of Nin... nine – whatever the name was – himself?" asked Whitby.

"Yes," agreed Caravan Bear. "Why did God need to send someone to do the dirty work for him?"

Christopher Rabbit scratched his head. "I expect God had his reasons," he said at last. "Anyway, Jonah didn't like the idea at all. Not one little bit.

"He'd heard of Nineveh, you see. It was the capital of the great Assyrian Empire and they were enemies of Jonah's people. Jonah really, really didn't want to go there."

"What was he supposed to do when he got there anyway?" asked Hector.

"Perhaps stand in the marketplace with a large placard around his neck shouting that God was angry with them?" suggested Whitby.

"He'd probably have been beaten and thrown out of the gates if he'd done that," Christopher Rabbit replied.

"Or he might have been beaten and killed and *then* thrown out of the gates," Whitby added.

Caravan Bear reeled in his line. A small piece of weed dangled on the end. He sighed and cast it out once more, further into the river.

"I wouldn't have wanted to go to Nine... that place," said Whitby. "Not if it was as bad as all that."

"Jonah might have thought that God didn't mean it when he said he'd destroy the city and kill all the people. He knew that God was kind and merciful," Christopher Rabbit continued.

"So are you saying that if he was standing in the marketplace with a large placard around his neck shouting that God was angry, the people of wherever it was might not have believed him?" asked Whitby.

"They might have just laughed at him," Hector said.

"Or perhaps beaten him and *then* laughed at him."

"Well, I think he was just plain scared," said Caravan Bear.

"I'd have been," Whitby agreed.

"So would I," Christopher Rabbit added.

"I wouldn't have gone," said Hector. "I'd have harnessed up my caravan and made off in the opposite direction. That's what *I'd* have done."

Christopher Rabbit nodded. "That's exactly what Jonah did do," he said. "Not harness up his caravan, because he didn't have one. But he didn't go to Nineveh. Instead he caught a ship going in the opposite direction."

"I bet God wasn't pleased about that," said Whitby.

"I bet he wasn't," Hector nodded.

"Well, I imagine God expected it," Christopher Rabbit replied, "because he knew what Jonah was like. But God couldn't have been too happy, because he sent a great storm.

"Not just any old storm that you might get when you're on a ship, but a really dreadful storm with wind howling around and rain lashing down and thunder roaring and lightning striking and huge, huge waves."

"I'd be seasick," said Whitby.

"How do you know?" asked Caravan Bear. "You've never been on a ship."

"No, but I get caravan sick when Hector goes too fast, so I expect it's the same."

"I never go too fast," Hector protested.

"Yes you do," Whitby replied.

"No I don't," said Hector.

"All the sailors were sick," said Christopher Rabbit hurriedly, trying to stop an argument from developing. "They were terrified. So was Jonah. The sailors wanted to find out who was to blame for the storm, so they wrote down the names of everyone on board, then drew out one name. It was Jonah's. They dragged him out of his cabin.

"'I know it's all my fault,' Jonah said. 'God asked me to go to Nineveh but I tried to run away – only you can't run away from God. There's only one way to stop the storm. You'll have to throw me overboard into the sea.'"

"Wow!" Whitby cried. "That sounds a bit drastic."

"It was brave of Jonah to say that," said Caravan Bear thoughtfully. "I don't think I would have."

"I'd have kept my head down and hoped it would all pass over," agreed Hector.

"So would I," said Christopher Rabbit. "It only goes to show that God knows us better than we think."

Everyone was silent for a bit.

"What happened next?" asked Whitby.

Christopher Rabbit looked down at his book. "The sailors threw him overboard."

"And did the storm stop?" asked Caravan Bear.

"Oh yes," replied Christopher Rabbit. "The storm stopped straightaway. The sea grew calm and the sun came out."

"And did Jonah drown?" asked Hector.

Christopher Rabbit shook his head. "No."

"Why?"

"Perhaps he could swim," suggested Caravan Bear.

"I don't know if he could swim or not," said Christopher Rabbit. "What happened was that he got swallowed up by a whale."

"He got WHAT?" demanded Whitby.

"He got swallowed by a whale," said Christopher Rabbit. "Well, it actually says a big fish in the story – but I expect it was a whale."

"Could have been a dolphin," said Caravan Bear wisely.

"Or a shark," said Hector.

"Or a sea monster," said Whitby.

"Let's call it a whale," said Christopher Rabbit firmly.

"Was he chewed up into little pieces?" Whitby asked, her eyes big and round.

"That's the funny thing," said Christopher Rabbit.

"He wasn't chewed up at all. It seems he just floated in past the whale's teeth and went straight into its stomach."

"Uggh," said Whitby, wrinkling up his nose.

"Nasty," agreed Hector.

"What happened next?" asked Caravan Bear, who had forgotten all about fishing.

"For three days and three nights Jonah stayed inside the whale."

"Bet he was hungry," said Caravan Bear.

"Oh, I don't know," said Hector, "he could have eaten the bits of fish that the whale hadn't digested. Kind of second-hand food."

"I don't fancy the sound of that," Whitby commented.

"If you're starving, you'll eat anything," insisted Caravan Bear.

That reminded Whitby. "I *am* pretty starving, so would you mind getting on with some fishing?" she asked Caravan Bear.

"Sorry."

"After three days and three nights the whale landed on a beach, and Jonah came out of the whale."

"How?" demanded Hector.

"I expect the whale was sick," said Christopher Rabbit.

"Did he come out in one piece?" asked Whitby.

"Yes," Christopher Rabbit answered. "Although I imagine he was a bit dirty."

Whitby wrinkled her nose. "I expect he smelled fishy."

"If I'd been him, I'd have had a wash," said Hector.

"No, you wouldn't," said Caravan Bear. "You don't like washing."

"Not usually," agreed Hector. "But if I'd just been thrown up by a whale, I think I'd have liked a wash then."

"So what happened after Jonah got out of the whale and had a wash?" asked Whitby.

"Did he go to Nineveh?" Hector added.

"Yes," said Christopher Rabbit. "He told God he was sorry he had disobeyed him, and set off for Nineveh."

"How did he know which way to go?" demanded Hector. "If he'd just been thrown up by a whale on some island or other in the middle of the sea, he'd have had a bit of a job knowing where Nineveh was. And it doesn't sound as if there was anyone around to ask directions."

"Perhaps he had a compass," said Whitby.

"Or a satnav," suggested Hector.

"Perhaps God showed him the way," said Caravan Bear.

"However it was, he managed to find the way," said Christopher Rabbit, "and when he got there, Jonah found that God was right. The people were wicked and cruel and had forgotten all about God.

"It wasn't an easy job, but in the end Jonah got his message over. From the king himself to the smallest child, everyone in the city was sorry. They asked God to forgive them and said that they would follow God's way in future. God was pleased because he didn't have to destroy the city."

"And I expect Jonah was pleased too," said Caravan Bear.

Whitby stood up. "That's it, job done – Jonah went home. And if only Caravan Bear had caught some fish, we could all go home to the caravan and have fish and chips for supper." Whitby was getting very hungry.

"Well, no," said Christopher Rabbit.

"What do you mean, no?"

"Jonah wasn't pleased at all," Christopher Rabbit continued.

"I'm not pleased either, as I don't think this river has any fish in it," said Whitby, sitting down again. "Or if it has, Caravan Bear hasn't found them."

"Why don't *you* have a go, then?" asked Caravan Bear. "It's not that easy to catch a fish."

"Unless you're Jonah," said Hector.

"That's different. That fish caught him."

Caravan Bear cast his line into the river again.

"Shall I go on?" asked Christopher Rabbit.

"Yes please," Whitby replied. "I expect it'll be a

long wait until we get something to eat."

"Right. Jonah wasn't pleased that God had decided not to destroy Nineveh. 'I knew this would happen,' he complained to God. 'When you told me to come here and tell them they'd all be wiped out in forty days if they didn't change their ways, I knew you wouldn't do it. You forgive people. All the time.

"'I ran away the first time because I knew that in the end you'd forgive them. I went through all that awful time in the storm – and then in the fish – and for what? Your trouble, God, if you don't mind my saying it, is that you always think the best of people.'"

Hector shook his head. "I don't think you should talk to God like that," he said.

"Why not?" asked Caravan Bear.

"Well, it's rude," said Hector. "God might not have liked it. He might have sent a thunderbolt or something to teach Jonah a lesson."

"Or he might have sent another fish who could have chewed Jonah into little pieces," said Whitby.

Christopher Rabbit looked in the book. "I don't think God minded Jonah talking to him like that. After all, Jonah had gone through a pretty bad time.

"Anyway, Jonah went on being angry. 'I think that

Nineveh crowd are a pretty awful lot, and you should have destroyed them,' he said. 'I'm sorry, but that's my opinion. I'm fed up. I really am. I wish I were dead.' He went out of the city, made a shelter for himself, sat in it, and sulked."

"I think Jonah had a point," said Hector slowly. "I mean, if God had decided at the beginning that he wouldn't destroy the city, why did he put Jonah through all that trouble?"

"But a lot of the trouble was Jonah's own fault," Caravan Bear commented. "If he'd done what God asked him in the first place, he would never have ended up inside the whale."

"And God *might* have destroyed the city if Jonah hadn't gone there in the end and got them to change their minds," suggested Whitby.

"God made a big shady bush grow over Jonah's shelter – it protected him from the blazing sun while Jonah slept. He slept all that day and the rest of the night. But God sent a worm to nibble away at the bush and it withered away."

"Why did God do that?" asked Whitby.

"Perhaps to teach Jonah a lesson," said Christopher Rabbit. "Jonah woke up the next morning sweltering under a really hot sun. He was very angry."

"Well, you would be if you'd just woken up. I'm often angry first thing in the morning, especially if I've been having a nice dream," said Caravan Bear.

"I expect he was hungry, too," added Whitby, looking at Caravan Bear.

"'I really think I'd be better off dead,' Jonah grumbled. 'I can see I'm no use to you, God, or to anyone else. And now that lovely bush has died – and it's such a shame. It was a beautiful bush and it kept me nice and cool. Now I'll get burned in this sun.'"

A cloud passed across the sun and everyone shivered.

"Getting cold," said Whitby.

"Getting late," said Hector.

"Getting hungry," added Whitby.

Caravan Bear suddenly remembered that he was supposed to be catching fish for their supper and cast his line once more into the water.

"What happened then?" asked Hector.

"God spoke to Jonah," Christopher Rabbit replied.

"I bet he was angry with him now," said Whitby.

"No, he wasn't. More sad, I'd say," Christopher Rabbit continued. "'Jonah,' God said. 'You're angry because the bush that gave you shelter has died, yet you did nothing to make it grow or keep it alive. So how do you expect me to feel about the thought of destroying a whole city – killing hundreds of thousands of people who I've made and cared for?

"'I know you think of them as your enemies – and you're frightened of them – but I think of them as my children, and I want them to know me, as you do. They might have been foolish and slow to learn right from wrong until you told them, but don't you think I should pity them and spare them?'"

Christopher Rabbit closed the book. "And that's the end of the story."

The animals were silent for a moment.

"That's a good story," said Whitby.

"What happened to Jonah?" asked Hector.

"I don't know," said Christopher Rabbit.

Caravan Bear carefully reeled in his line and stood up. "Sorry, everyone. No fish tonight. How about egg and chips instead?"

After they had eaten their supper, Christopher Rabbit went down to the riverbank and looked at the kingfishers darting among the reeds, bright in the evening sun.

"It can't be easy to love our enemies and care for those we don't like," he thought. "Poor old Jonah. But God loves and cares for everyone."

Suddenly the sun dipped below the horizon and dark shadows began to form. The riverbank suddenly looked strange and a bit frightening. Christopher Rabbit shivered.

"Please, God, give me courage when I'm afraid," he said out loud. Then he turned and began to walk back to the caravan.

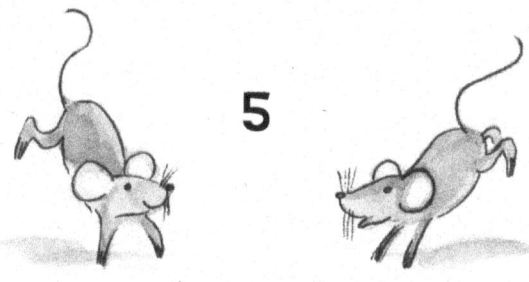

5

The Babbling Tower

"I know – let's hold a party," said Caravan Bear one afternoon.

"Why?" asked Whitby, who was busy chasing some field mice round and round the caravan.

"Because we've made a lot of new friends while we've been staying here," Caravan Bear replied, "and we've been invited into their homes, so it's only right we should invite them back – especially as we'll soon be moving on."

The friends had stayed in the farmer's field longer than they had first thought they would, as they had been enjoying themselves. But as Caravan Bear had said, "We're on holiday, so we can stay as long or as short a time as we want."

And everyone had agreed.

THE JOURNEY BEGINS

"We'll soon be moving on, will we?" asked Hector, who was grazing on the fresh green grass in the field where the caravan was parked. "I like it here."

"So do I, but the farmer said he needs to plough the field and plant crops, so I said we'd be going."

"All right," said Whitby. "I'll invite the field mice to the party."

"And you can help me with the food," suggested Caravan Bear.

"I'll write the invitations," Christopher Rabbit offered.

So Caravan Bear and Whitby prepared mountains of food while Christopher Rabbit, who had the best handwriting, wrote out invitations and Hector delivered them.

They lit candles in and around the caravan as it grew dark, and soon their friends began to arrive. Barney and Erica, two hedgehogs, were the first, quickly followed by Belinda the blackbird and Mavis the owl.

Soon the caravan was bursting with animals. Freddie the fox brought a harmonica and Caravan Bear fetched his guitar, and they sat playing songs and singing. No one listened to them though because

they were all talking, laughing, and eating.

After a while, the noise grew so loud that the farmer came out of his house, walked across the field, and knocked on the caravan door. He had to knock quite hard as, by this time, the sounds inside were very loud indeed – the party had been joined by six field mice, four chickens, and Daphne the goose.

At last Caravan Bear heard the banging.

"Can't you pipe down?" the farmer shouted. "My wife and I can't sleep with all the racket you're making!"

"Sorry," said Caravan Bear. "We've having a party. Would you and your wife like to come and join us?"

"No, we wouldn't," said the farmer. "I've got to be up early to get on with milking the cows, and that's another thing. You've woken them up, too, and they're making a terrible noise."

"I'll tell everyone to be quiet," Caravan Bear promised. He turned back inside and called out, "QUIET EVERYONE!"

"A right old Tower of Babel you've got in there," the farmer grumbled as he walked down the steps of the caravan and back to his house.

"What's the Tower of Babel?" asked Belinda.

"We'd better be getting back to the forest," said Barney and Erica.

Freddie put away his harmonica and stood up. "I'd best go too."

"Oh, please don't go," urged Caravan Bear. "It's not late."

"Can't we do something quiet?" asked Whitby.

"Like what?"

"Would you like me to tell you a story from the Bible?" asked Christopher Rabbit.

"Is there one about that tower the farmer mentioned?" Belinda asked. "I'd like to know what it is."

Christopher Rabbit looked through his book. "Yes, there is."

"What did the farmer call it?"

"Babel. It's the story of the Tower of Babel."

Caravan Bear refilled everyone's glasses while the animals and birds settled themselves comfortably on every available space – some sitting, some lying, some perching.

"There once was a time when everyone in the world spoke the same language. They had been wandering around for many years…"

"Like us," Hector interrupted.

"… looking for somewhere to settle – somewhere with good land to grow their crops, fresh water, and good weather. At last they found a place and decided to make it their home."

"'Let's build a tower,' one of the people suggested. 'A tall tower – a really enormous one that will reach to the sky.'"

"Why?" asked Belinda.

"What do you mean, why?"

"Why build a tower? I build a nest each year for myself and my chicks, but I don't see much point in building a tower unless you're going to use it for something."

"They might have wanted to see the view from the top," suggested Mavis the owl. "Of course, we birds don't have that problem."

"I don't think they wanted to build a tower to use it for anything," Christopher Rabbit said. "I think they did it to show that they were clever enough to do it."

"It's just the kind of stupid thing humans do," said Whitby; "build a perfectly useless tower."

"Who did they want to impress?" Mavis hooted.

"Well, God, I suppose," said Christopher Rabbit.

"Because once they started building, they decided that they would build it higher and higher to reach the heavens. I think they wanted to show God that they were as important as him. So they made bricks to build it with, and built it higher and higher until its top was lost in the clouds."

"That made it a bit dangerous for birds," Belinda added. "You could easily crash into it when flying."

"I don't suppose they thought of that," Christopher Rabbit shrugged.

Hector, who had been quietly munching some oats, suddenly said, "So are you saying that they wanted to build the tower high enough so that they could reach heaven?"

"What's heaven?" asked Barney.

"Heaven's where God is, isn't it?" Hector replied uncertainly.

"And is it up in the sky?"

"Is God up in the sky?" asked Whitby.

"Probably," said Caravan Bear. He turned to the rabbit. "What do you think?"

Christopher Rabbit thought for a moment. "I'm not sure heaven and God are in any particular place," he said at last. "I think God is everywhere."

"You mean here? In our caravan?" Whitby whispered. "At our party?"

"Why not?"

Whitby looked around the packed caravan. "Not much room, is there?"

All the animals looked around as if they expected to see God sitting in a corner of the caravan.

"I've flown very high," said Belinda, "and never seen heaven... or God, for that matter," she added.

Christopher Rabbit went on with the story. "'If we reach heaven we'll be as important as God,' one of the men boasted.

"'More important,' said another."

"No one can be more important than God, because God made us," Caravan Bear objected.

"I don't think they thought of that when they started building," said Christopher Rabbit.

"But wouldn't it be nice to find heaven?" said Belinda.

"I don't think so," said Mavis. "I think it would be stupid to even try."

"Why?"

"Because heaven is where God is – and if he wants us to see it, we will, and if he doesn't, we won't. Same with God. If he wants us to see him, we will. It all seems pretty obvious to me."

"But…" began Belinda.

"You don't see the wind, do you?" said Mavis. "You feel it in your wings when you fly, but you can't point to something and say, 'That's the wind.' I think it's the same with God."

"Go on with the story," urged Hector.

"Well, the people built and built and the tower grew higher and higher. The view from the top was wonderful."

"No better than when I'm flying," Mavis sniffed.

"Soon you couldn't see the top of the tower from the ground," said Christopher Rabbit.

"I bet God had something to say about that," said Whitby.

"He did. When he saw what they were doing, he realized that the people had become so full of their own importance that they thought they were more important than him. So God decided to teach them a lesson."

Christopher Rabbit stopped to take a sip of his drink.

"Go on," squeaked one of the field mice. "What did he do?"

"Something quite clever. He muddled up their language."

"What do you mean?" squeaked the mouse.

"He made them all speak in different languages so that they couldn't understand each other."

"Neat," said Whitby.

"So when one person said, 'Mind out or a brick will fall on your head!' the person underneath didn't understand and didn't get out of the way."

"And the brick fell on his head."

"Yes. You can imagine what happened. Everyone began arguing and shouting and fighting because they couldn't understand what anyone else was saying."

"I bet God was having a good laugh about it," said Belinda.

"It taught the people a lesson. They gave up work on the tower and gradually it began to fall to bits. Everyone moved away."

"So that's how people have different languages," said Whitby.

"And live in different countries," added Caravan Bear.

"I expect so," said Christopher Rabbit. "Nothing was left except a pile of bricks, which, in the end, turned into the dust of the desert."

The animals were silent for a while. The candles flickered and began to go out. Mavis hooted.

"I must be off."

But no one made a move to go as it was warm and comfortable inside.

"So why was it called the Tower of Babel?" asked Whitby sleepily.

"Perhaps because the people all made a babble of different noises," said Christopher Rabbit. He was tired and wished everyone would go home so he could go to bed.

Everyone stood up or flew down and began to leave, thanking Caravan Bear, Whitby, Christopher Rabbit, and Hector for a lovely party.

"Ssh!" warned Caravan Bear. "We don't want to wake the farmer or his wife."

When everyone had gone, the friends decided to clear up the mess in the morning and go straight to bed. But first Christopher Rabbit went out on to the steps of the caravan and looked up at the clear, starlit sky.

THE BABBLING TOWER

"Wherever you are, God – up in the sky, all around us, or inside our caravan – thank you for looking after us."

And he went inside, closed the door, and went to bed.

6

Noah and the Flood

"Rain, rain, nothing but rain," complained Whitby, her nose pressed against the window, as she watched the rain falling in a steady stream outside the caravan. She sighed. "When's it going to stop?"

Just as she said that, there was a loud, grinding noise and the caravan, which had been moving slowly along the road pulled by a very wet Hector, suddenly stopped with a jolt. Whitby, Caravan Bear, and Christopher Rabbit were thrown on to the floor; plates, cups, and saucers fell off their shelves on top of them.

"What's happened?" asked Caravan Bear. He struggled to his feet and pulled open the door. Wind and rain rushed inside.

"Close the door," shouted Whitby. "We're getting soaked!"

"Not as soaked as me," said Hector, putting his nose inside the van. "We've stopped."

"We know that," said Whitby, rubbing her head, sore from where a cup had hit it.

"Why have we stopped?" asked Caravan Bear, peering down the caravan steps. The steps ended in a large puddle. No, it was bigger than a puddle – it was a small lake that spread right across the road. The

bottom step of the caravan was under water, and so were its bright yellow wheels.

"I didn't think it was so deep," said Hector unhappily. "I thought I could pull the caravan through."

"Well, you thought wrong," said Whitby angrily. "It was a stupid thing to do."

"It's all right for you, nice and dry and cosy inside! I'm wet and I'm cold and I've had enough!" Hector retorted.

"Why are you taking us this way anyway?" asked Whitby, whose head was hurting.

Hector shrugged. "It's as good a way as any other."

"Stop arguing about it," said Caravan Bear. "What are we going to do?"

"Stay here until it's stopped raining and the water's gone down," replied Hector. "We can't do much else."

"Can we help push the caravan out?" asked Christopher Rabbit, who had been replacing the cups and saucers on their shelves.

"We'll only get soaked," Whitby grumbled.

"And we might damage the caravan." Caravan Bear looked worried. "I think Hector's right. We've just got to stay here. Here's a blanket for you, Hector, and some oats. It's not your fault."

So the friends sat in the caravan as the rain hammered down on the roof and the water rose higher and higher.

"Can anyone swim?" asked Whitby after a while. "I can't."

"Nor me," said Caravan Bear.

They were all quiet for a while, listening to the rain.

"It always sounds worse in the caravan," said Caravan Bear reassuringly. "It's probably not so bad outside."

"Yes it is," said Hector, poking his nose in through the door. "It's a lot worse."

"Perhaps the caravan will float, like Noah's ark," said Christopher Rabbit.

"What's Noah's ark?" asked Whitby.

"It's a kind of wooden boat God told Noah to build when he sent a flood," said Christopher Rabbit. "It's a story in the Bible."

"Why don't you tell us about it?" asked Caravan Bear. "It'll help take our minds off the weather."

"Not if it's about a flood," said Whitby gloomily.

"Can't you tell us a happy story about a sunny day?"

"Does it have a happy ending?" asked Hector. "I like happy endings."

"Well, yes," said Christopher Rabbit. "It does have a happy ending. But it's a bit sad as well."

"What's that meant to mean?" Whitby demanded.

"It starts sad but ends happy," Christopher Rabbit replied.

"Better than starting happy – like we did when we went off this morning with the sun shining – and ending unhappy, like now," said Hector. He sniffed. "And I think I've caught a cold."

"Tell us the story," said Caravan Bear.

Christopher Rabbit picked up the Bible, which, like everything else, had fallen on the floor, and found the right page.

"When Noah was a very old man, God spoke to him. He told him that because people had grown so wicked, he was going to send a flood and destroy everything."

"Everything?" squeaked Whitby.

"Everything."

"Couldn't God have thought of something a bit less drastic?" Caravan Bear said.

"I'm sure he could have, but he didn't," said Christopher Rabbit.

Whitby looked at the rain streaming past the windows and listened to it drumming on the roof.

"Do you think that's what God's doing now?" she asked in a frightened whisper. "Sending a flood to drown us all?"

"No," said Christopher Rabbit.

"How do you know?" asked Whitby.

"Because I've read the end of the story."

"Get on with it, then," said Hector. "I want to hear how it ended."

Christopher Rabbit looked down at the Bible. "God said that he would save him, his wife, his three sons and their wives, and two of every animal."

"Why did God say he'd save Noah?" asked Whitby.

"He said it was because Noah was the only good man in the world. Everyone else was wicked. He told Noah to build an ark…"

"I wish this caravan was an ark," said Caravan Bear.

"Bit of a tight squeeze, if the ark were like this caravan," said Whitby, looking around.

"It was a bit bigger than this caravan," said Christopher Rabbit. "God gave Noah exact measurements. He said it was to be a hundred and thirty-three metres long..."

"Don't tell us," said Hector. "Figures have always made my head ache."

"Was Noah a carpenter if God told him to build the ark?" asked Whitby.

"Or a sailor?" added Caravan Bear.

"No, he was a farmer. He grew grapes and made wine."

"Fat lot of use that would be on an ark," said Whitby. "Wouldn't it have been better if God had chosen a carpenter or a sailor?"

"I don't think it mattered what work Noah did," Caravan Bear said thoughtfully. "I expect that what mattered was that he was a good man."

"God said that it would rain for forty days and forty nights..." Christopher Rabbit went on.

"Like now," said Whitby gloomily.

"... until the world was flooded, but Noah and all

the animals would be saved."

Everyone was quiet for a moment, then Whitby suddenly asked, "What about fish?"

"What about fish?"

"God didn't mention fish, did he?"

Christopher Rabbit thought about it. "There wasn't any need," he said at last.

"Why not?"

"Because fish can swim, so they didn't need saving from a flood."

"Just imagine all those animals being shut up on board the ark… the smell…!" Caravan Bear wrinkled his nose.

"Just think of two lions…" Whitby began.

"… shut up with two lambs," Caravan Bear went on.

"Why didn't they eat each other?" asked Hector, munching a bowlful of oats.

Christopher Rabbit looked in the Bible. "God told Noah to take enough food for everyone," he said.

"Sensible," said Caravan Bear.

"Spiders!" Whitby shrieked, having spotted one hanging down from a shelf. She tried to swat it away and missed.

"What's wrong with spiders?" asked Caravan Bear.

"I'm scared of them," said Whitby.

"Why's that?"

"They look horrid."

"I expect you look horrid to a spider," said Christopher Rabbit.

"So what happened next?" asked Caravan Bear.

"And snakes," Whitby interrupted. "I've never liked snakes, and I like them even less after what one of them did in the Garden of Eden."

Christopher Rabbit thought about it. "I don't think God takes sides like that," he said at last. "I don't think he says, 'Don't like the look of you, so you're not going on the ark – you can drown.'"

"He did that to all the wicked people," said Hector.

"Well, I'm not God so I don't know the answer," replied Christopher Rabbit irritably. "Anyway, Noah finished the ark, got all the animals on board, closed the door, and it began to rain."

"Like now."

"Much worse. It rained and it rained and it rained," said Christopher Rabbit. "The ark began to float and soon all the land was covered with water. Everyone was shut up in the ark until the rain stopped."

"Woodpeckers!" said Whitby suddenly.

"What about woodpeckers?"

"They peck wood, don't they? So didn't the ark leak?"

"The story doesn't say. But even if it did leak, it didn't sink." Christopher Rabbit went on. "When it stopped raining…"

"After forty days…" said Whitby.

"… and forty nights…" Hector added. "You see, we *have* been listening."

"Noah couldn't open the doors of the ark because everyone would have fallen in the water and drowned. He had to wait, as the water kept going down for a hundred and fifty days."

"I bet they were all pretty bored by that time," said Caravan Bear. "I hope they'd taken some games into the ark with them. We've got a cupboard full of games in our caravan," he added proudly.

Whitby wrinkled her nose. "I bet it was even more smelly in the ark by then."

"God sent a wind that made the waters go down, and the ark landed at the top of a mountain called Ararat. Then Noah had a good idea – he let a raven fly out of the ark."

"Good move," said Caravan Bear approvingly. "I expect he thought that the raven would fly around and see whether there was enough land for everyone to leave the ark without falling into the water."

"The raven flew away and didn't come back, so Noah sent out a dove. After flying around for a bit the dove came back, shaking her head. There was still too much water. A few days later, she flew off again. This time she came back to the ark with a fresh olive leaf in her beak."

"Was that good?" asked Hector, who was not feeling at all well. He sneezed suddenly.

"Yes – it was good. It meant that the water had gone down so far that the tops of the trees were out of the water. And after another few days, Noah opened the door of the ark and everyone came out."

"Phew, I bet they were glad!" said Whitby.

"I bet they were," agreed Caravan Bear.

"Is that the end of the story?" asked Hector.

"Not quite. God told Noah that he would never again send a flood to destroy the world. He said that whenever there was a rainbow in the sky, he would remember his promise."

"Listen!" said Whitby. Everyone was silent.

THE JOURNEY BEGINS

"It's stopped raining!" cried Christopher Rabbit.

Caravan Bear opened the door of the caravan. "Not quite. But the water's already starting to go down," he said. "We won't be stuck here for much longer."

Christopher Rabbit came to the door. The sun had come out from behind a cloud, its light reflecting against the rain. He looked up and gasped. High above him he could see glowing bands – red, orange, yellow, green, blue, indigo, and violet – banded together in the perfect arc of a rainbow.

"Thank you, God," he said, "for keeping your promise."

He ducked back inside the caravan. "Come and look, everyone! It's beautiful out here!"

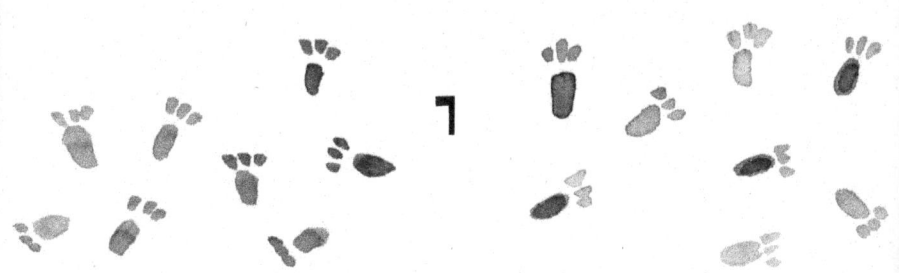

Joseph and His Brothers

The little pig stood up. "Hello," he said.

"What are you doing here?" asked Caravan Bear.

"The door was open, so I came in," said the piglet.

"It would have been polite to knock first," said Christopher Rabbit.

"I did. No one answered."

"That's because we were out," said Whitby.

Caravan Bear looked around. The inside of the caravan was a mess. Crumbs were strewn across the floor, Whitby's favourite cushion had been squashed, and there were sticky paw prints all over the table.

"Who are you?" asked Caravan Bear.

"I'm Runt."

"Runt."

"That's right. When I was born the farmer said,

'Runt of the litter,' so that's what I was called."

"But 'runt' means small," said Christopher Rabbit.

"That's me. Small and best." Runt stared up at the friends, a beaming smile on his face.

"Born last and best of all my brothers and sisters," he went on. "That's what Mother says. My brothers and sisters are useless."

"Is that what your mother said? That your brothers and sisters are useless?" asked Whitby, disbelieving.

Runt smiled smugly. "No. That's what *I* say. They're only good for the chop."

"What do you mean?" asked Hector, who was peering in through the window.

"Sausages," said Runt. "But not me – I'm too clever for that."

The animals looked at one another.

"You've eaten the cake we were going to have for tea," said Whitby angrily.

"Sorry about that," said Runt. But he didn't look at all sorry.

"Never mind," said Caravan Bear. "Perhaps you were hungry. Now you're here, would you like some tea?"

"It'll only be a cup," said Whitby gloomily. "No cake."

"And Christopher Rabbit was going to read us a story."

Christopher Rabbit took down the Bible and looked at Runt. "I was going to read you a story about a journey but I think I'd better tell you about Joseph instead."

"Why?"

"You'll see."

Everyone settled down with cups of tea and some biscuits Caravan Bear had found. "They're stale but it's all we've got," he said with a look at Runt.

Christopher Rabbit opened the book. "This is a

story about someone called Joseph. Now, Joseph had a lot of troubles in his life that he overcame with God's help, and he ended up a very important person."

"Like me," said Runt.

"Joseph's first trouble was that he was one of the youngest in the family. He didn't have just one older brother, or two, or three…"

"… or four?" asked Whitby.

Christopher Rabbit shook his head.

"… five?" asked Hector. Again Christopher Rabbit shook his head.

"… six?" asked Caravan Bear.

"I've got six brothers and two sisters," said Runt importantly.

"He had ten older brothers and one older sister," said Christopher Rabbit. "It was a big family. Just think of it. Ten brothers and one older sister all bossing him around and treating him like a baby."

"No one treats me like a baby," said Runt.

"I'm sure they don't," said Caravan Bear.

"I'm sure they daren't," said Whitby.

Before Runt could reply, Christopher Rabbit continued. "His next trouble was that his mother,

Rachel, had wanted a baby for a long time, so he was very special to her. She might have spoiled him."

"Why did she want another baby if she already had all those before Joseph?" asked Hector.

"They weren't her children. They were the sons and daughter of other women," said Christopher Rabbit. "Joseph's next trouble was that not only did his mother spoil him, but his father did, too."

"I don't get spoiled," Runt added.

"Jacob, who was Joseph's father, was a very wealthy man. He owned cattle, sheep, goats, camels, all kinds of animals. They lived in the country and his sons herded the cattle, looked after the sheep, and worked long hours on the farm."

"I bet Joseph didn't," said Whitby.

"Why not?" asked Hector.

"Because he was spoiled," said Whitby.

"I'm not spoiled," said Runt again. "I don't do any hard work either, but then neither do my brothers or sisters. All they do is wander around the pigsty looking for food. I don't need to do that as my mother gives me plenty to eat."

Caravan Bear and Whitby exchanged looks.

"Joseph was the apple of his father's eye. He gave

him everything he wanted, including a wonderful coat woven from many different wools. It had long, wide sleeves. His brothers didn't like that. They only had ordinary, rough shepherds' coats with no sleeves.

"So Joseph's next trouble was that his brothers were jealous of him. Partly because his mother and father loved him best, but also because he wasn't like his brothers."

"He might have been quiet," said Hector.

"How would you know?" asked Whitby.

"I'm quiet," said Hector.

"Except when you're towing the caravan," murmured Caravan Bear.

"Well, he might have been good-looking," said Hector, tossing back his mane.

"I'm good-looking," said Runt.

"Perhaps he was clever," said Whitby.

"That's me," said Runt.

"He had dreams," said Christopher Rabbit.

"I have dreams," said Runt importantly.

"So do we all, but Joseph's dreams were unusual. Unfortunately he told his brothers about them, which wasn't a very sensible thing to do."

"Why not?" asked Caravan Bear.

"In one of his dreams he and his brothers were binding together sheaves of corn. Joseph's sheaf of corn stood up by itself and his brothers' sheaves all bowed down before it. His brothers didn't like that."

Whitby looked confused. "Why not?"

"It's obvious," said Runt. "His brothers thought that Joseph was telling them that they'd have to bow down to him."

No one said anything.

Christopher Rabbit went on. "Joseph had another dream. He told his brothers that the sun, the moon, and eleven stars would all bow down to him."

"I bet they didn't like that," said Caravan Bear.

"They didn't. Even his father was angry with him. 'What kind of dream is that?' he asked. 'Are you telling me that all your family will have to bow down before you?'"

"I'd like to have dreams like that," said Runt.

"I don't think you would," said Christopher Rabbit. "His brothers hated Joseph because of them."

"And because of the coat," said Whitby.

"Yes, because of his coat and because he was different."

"Not a good idea to be different," said Hector

gloomily. "I was different and I got beaten."

"Why?" asked Whitby.

"They said I was slow."

"Slow! They'd never seen you tow a caravan, then!"

"Go on with the story," said Caravan Bear.

"They probably also hated him because his parents loved him best," said Christopher Rabbit.

"Not a good idea for your mother and father to love one of their children more than the others," said Hector. Everyone looked at him but Hector didn't say any more.

"Mother loves me best," Runt said smugly. "I don't think my brothers and sisters like it, but who cares."

Everyone was silent for a moment.

"One day Jacob sent for Joseph and asked him to go and find his brothers, who were out looking after the sheep. They'd been gone a long time and Jacob was beginning to get worried.

"Joseph set off. At last he saw them, far in the distance. They saw him too. As he was dressed in his fine coat, they could hardly miss him.

"'Well well, just look who's coming,' said Judah, one of his brothers.

"'The dreamer,' said Dan and everyone laughed,

but not in a friendly way. They watched him approach. They were all hot and tired, and the sight of Joseph was the last straw.

"'I know,' said another brother suddenly. 'Now's our chance. He's all alone. Let's get rid of him.'

"'Good idea,' said a fourth. 'We'll kill him and throw his body into a pit!'

"'We can say that a wild beast attacked him,' Dan said enthusiastically. 'Then we'll see what comes of his dreams!' They all laughed.

"So they lay in wait, and when Joseph came up to them they jumped out, stripped him of his coat, and beat him."

"Did they kill him?" asked Whitby, wide-eyed.

By this time, Runt was looking a little uncomfortable. "Perhaps I ought to go," he said. "Mother and Father will be missing me."

"I've nearly finished," said Christopher Rabbit. "Do stay."

"Have another cup of tea," offered Caravan Bear.

"And another stale biscuit," said Whitby.

"Joseph's eldest brother was called Reuben," Christopher Rabbit continued. "He didn't like all this talk of killing."

"'Let's just toss him into a pit for a day or two to teach him a lesson,' Reuben pleaded. He had decided to rescue Joseph from the pit when the other brothers had gone."

"That was nice of him," said Hector.

"Well, yes – I suppose so," Caravan Bear replied. "But if he was the oldest, he could have stopped them beating him in the first place, couldn't he?"

"Not if it was just him against the rest," said Whitby.

Runt ate his stale biscuit and didn't say a word.

"His brothers finished beating Joseph and put him in the pit. It had steep walls and Joseph wouldn't have been able to get out without someone to help him. Reuben went off to find a sheep that had gone missing, and while he was gone, his brothers sat down and had a meal."

"I bet they didn't give any of it to Joseph," said Whitby.

"I shouldn't think they did," agreed Caravan Bear.

While they were eating, they saw a line of camels in the distance. The camels were being ridden by merchants who were on their way to Egypt. Judah had an idea. 'Let's sell Joseph to those merchants,' he said. 'Then we'll get rid of him without actually killing him ourselves.'

"'And we'll make some money at the same time,' said another brother eagerly.

"'Good plan,' said a third. The others all nodded their agreement, so they called out to the merchants. 'Here, do you want to buy this good-looking strong young lad?'

"'He'll fetch a good price in Egypt,' called another. 'You can have him for…' He looked at his brothers.

"'… thirty pieces of silver,' said Judah, and the merchants nodded.

"They dragged Joseph out of the pit. He was dazed, bruised, dirty, and very, very frightened. The merchants looked at him.

"'Twenty,' said one of them. 'He's not worth more than that.'

"The brothers agreed, the merchants paid the money, and Joseph was taken away in chains."

There was a shocked silence in the caravan.

"That's dreadful," said Whitby at last.

"To do that to your own brother," said Caravan Bear.

Runt shifted uneasily. "I bet my brothers and

sisters would do something like that to me if they could,' he said. "But they're not smart enough."

No one said anything.

"That's not the end of the story, is it?" asked Hector.

"Not nearly the end," said Christopher Rabbit. "We mustn't forget Joseph's oldest brother, Reuben. When he got back and found Joseph was no longer in the pit, he was very upset.

"'Where is he?' Reuben asked.

"'It's all right,' said Judah. 'Don't worry. We didn't kill him. He's still alive. We sold him to some merchants going to Egypt. Here you are – here's your share of the money.'

"Reuben was even more upset. 'You stupid fools,' he said. 'Have you thought about what we're going to tell Father? All right, we might not have liked Joseph, but this is terrible. He loves Joseph the best. It's a terrible thing you've done. He'll kill us all if he finds out.'

"The brothers looked at one another. They hadn't thought of that. Then one of them had an idea. He took Joseph's coat, tore it, and dipped it in some goat's blood, then they all went home.

"'Where's Joseph?' Jacob asked as soon as he saw them. 'I sent him to find you.'

"The brothers looked at one another. 'We haven't seen him,' Reuben lied. 'But we found this on our way home.' He held out the torn and bloody coat.

"Jacob took the coat and laid it across his knees. He wept and mourned. No one could comfort him.

"Meanwhile many hundreds of miles away, Joseph was sold in an Egyptian slave market."

Christopher Rabbit closed the book and stood up.

"So what happened?" asked Whitby.

"That's another story," Christopher Rabbit replied.

"Did it all work out all right?" Whitby demanded.

"Yes," said Christopher Rabbit, "in the end." He looked at Runt, who was sitting on the floor looking rather small and rather unhappy. "Isn't it time you went home?"

"Suppose so," said Runt. He stood up. "Just shows you how awful older brothers and sisters can be, doesn't it?"

"You could also say that Joseph deserved it," said Whitby.

"Not throwing him into a pit!" said Runt hotly. "Or selling him!"

"No, not that," said Christopher Rabbit gently. "But it really isn't a good idea to be boastful and think yourself better than everyone else, is it?"

Runt said nothing. He left the caravan without thanking Caravan Bear for the tea or saying he was sorry he had eaten all the cake.

"And all the biscuits!" Whitby pointed out.

"Yes, but they were stale," said Caravan Bear. "We'll buy some fresh ones in the morning."

"I hope Runt learns something from that story, God," Christopher Rabbit said as he climbed into his bed. "Help us all to learn something from it."

And he went to sleep.

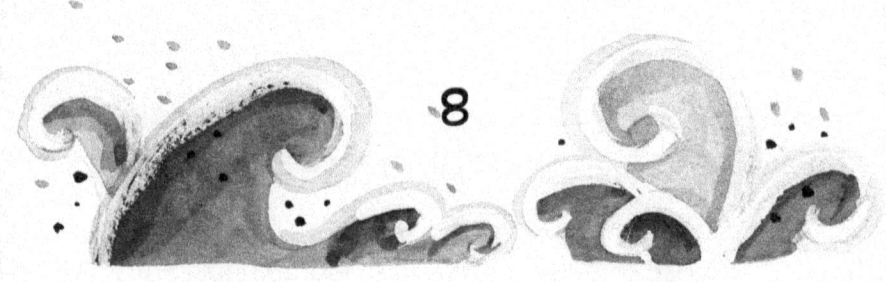

Crossing the Red Sea

Clip, clop, clip, clop.

Hector the horse towed the caravan smartly along the road.

Clip, clop, clip, clop.

As he went, he grumbled to himself. "I don't know where we're going. Caravan Bear said it will be worth it when we get there, but I'm tired and I want to stop."

He looked around. "Not much good grazing grass anyway. It's all rocks and bracken."

He flicked away some midges with his tail.

"It's all right for Caravan Bear, Whitby, and Christopher Rabbit," he thought. The three of them were sitting on the steps of the caravan enjoying the sunshine.

"I'm the one doing all the work."

He turned a corner and stopped so abruptly that Caravan Bear, Whitby, and Christopher Rabbit nearly fell off the steps.

"Oh!" said Hector.

He had reached the end of the road and there, in front of him, was a fine beach of golden sand. Beyond it was the sea, blue and sparkling in the sunshine.

"Well," said Caravan Bear, coming to stand beside Hector, "was it worth it?"

Whitby and Christopher Rabbit joined him.

"It's lovely!" Whitby, tail flying, rushed down to the water's edge, barking loudly while Caravan Bear and Christopher Rabbit unhitched Hector from the caravan. Whitby raced back.

"Is that the sea?" asked Christopher Rabbit. He had never been to the sea before.

"Yes," said Whitby. "Wonderful, isn't it?"

"Where does it end?"

"It goes right around the world, but there's lots of land in between."

"I've never seen anything like it," said Christopher Rabbit.

"I'll make some tea," said Caravan Bear and he climbed into the caravan.

"Hello," said a familiar voice.

Christopher Rabbit, Hector, and Whitby peered inside. Standing there, looking very pleased with himself, was Runt.

"What are you doing here?" Caravan Bear demanded.

"I stowed away."

"Where?"

"In the cupboard," said Runt.

"Why?" asked Whitby.

"Why not?"

"Won't you be missed?"

Runt shrugged. "Probably."

"Well, you can't stay here with us," said Whitby. "We never asked you, we don't want you, and you can just go home."

"I don't know the way," said Runt.

"You should have thought of that before you stowed away," said Hector.

"Look," said Caravan Bear, "let's have a cup of tea. You can stay with us until we go home, then we'll leave you at the farm."

Whitby ran off down to the water's edge again. Christopher Rabbit followed.

"It's all spoiled," said Whitby angrily.

"No, it's not," Christopher Rabbit protested.

"Yes, it is. He's horrible and selfish and none of us like him."

"Well we're stuck with him now, so we might as well make the best of it. He won't really be a bother and it's so beautiful here that he can't spoil that, can he?"

"He'll spoil anything."

"I'll tell you what," said Christopher Rabbit. "Would you like me to read a story from the Bible after supper?"

After supper everyone settled themselves on the beach as it was still warm, and Christopher Rabbit opened the Bible.

"This story is called 'Crossing the Red Sea'," said Christopher Rabbit. "The Israelites – who were God's people - were slaves in Egypt."

"How do you mean they were God's people?" asked Whitby.

"God had made them a promise that he would always look after them and care for them."

"Like he does for us?"

"Yes," agreed Christopher Rabbit. "Like he does for us."

"Why did you call them Israelites?" asked Hector.

"Because they were people of the land of Israel. They'd been taken away from their homes and made slaves."

"So what's a slave?"

Christopher Rabbit thought for a moment. "It's someone who is owned by someone else and has to work for them." He looked around at the others. "Let's say Caravan Bear had bought you, Hector, so you wouldn't be able to just leave if you didn't like what Caravan Bear asked you to do."

"I didn't buy you to own you, Hector," Caravan Bear explained. "I paid money for you so that you can be free. If you don't like towing the caravan, you don't have to."

Hector thought about this. "I don't always like what you ask me to do," he said. "Especially when it means towing the caravan through the rain."

"Yes, but you don't have to do it. You could just say, 'Sorry, I'm not towing the caravan until the rain stops.' Or you could just leave."

"I wouldn't do that," said Hector. "You've been very good to me. You rescued me from a nasty owner who bought me from another farmer and then beat me."

"Well, there you are," said Christopher Rabbit. "You know what it's like to have been a slave."

Hector nodded and returned to nibbling the grass dotted around the sand dunes.

"The slaves led a horrible life and prayed that God would rescue them and give them a land of their own. God listened and chose a man called Moses to be their leader. He told Moses to go to the king of Egypt and demand that he free the slaves.

"Moses wasn't at all keen at being given the job. He told God he couldn't do it. He said he wasn't good at talking and people wouldn't listen to him. He asked God to choose someone else to be in charge."

"Why did he do that?" asked Whitby.

"Perhaps he was frightened," said Caravan Bear.

"I wouldn't be frightened," boasted Runt.

"You would if God had chosen you instead of Moses."

"No, I wouldn't," said Runt. "I'm not frightened of anything."

"Well, you weren't in Egypt at the time, otherwise God might have chosen differently," said Christopher Rabbit peaceably. "Anyway, God said that Moses could take his brother Aaron with him to do the talking as Aaron was a good speaker."

"So why didn't God choose Aaron instead of Moses?" asked Whitby.

Hector suddenly looked up.

"It's a bit like Jonah, isn't it?" he said. "He didn't want to do what God asked him either."

"Did Moses end up inside a big fish, like Jonah?" asked Whitby eagerly.

"No. Moses didn't run away like Jonah. He said he'd do what God had asked him. He went to the king of Egypt and told him: 'The God of Israel wants you to free his people.'"

"I bet that didn't go down well," said Caravan Bear.

"It didn't," Christopher Rabbit agreed. "'Who is this God?' the king asked. 'I don't know him and I don't see why I should do what he wants!' He was very angry and took it out on the Israelites, making their lives even worse than they had been before."

"I don't suppose Moses went about it the right way," said Runt. "You don't just talk to kings as if they were anyone."

"I suppose you've met lots of kings," said Whitby sarcastically.

Runt shrugged. "Stands to reason," he said. "I don't like the farmer but I'm always nice and polite when I see him."

"Pity you're not nice and polite to us, then," Whitby muttered.

"Anyway, Moses told God what the king had said, although of course God knew already, and God promised Moses that he would make the king change his mind. And he did. Ten terrible disasters came to Egypt."

"What were they?" asked Runt eagerly.

"First God turned the water of the River Nile to blood, which meant that the water smelled horrible, the fish died, and no one had any fresh water to drink."

Christopher Rabbit, Caravan Bear, Whitby, and Hector looked across at the calm blue sea.

"Nasty," said Caravan Bear.

"Very nasty," said Whitby.

"Just imagine what it would be like if the sea turned red," said Runt, looking as if he rather liked the idea.

"What happened then...?" asked Hector.

"Then Moses went back to the king and asked him once more to free the Israelite slaves, but the King refused."

"And...?"

"All the frogs who lived on the riverbank came hopping into the towns and ended up in everyone's houses, their beds, even their ovens."

"What's wrong with that? I like frogs," said Whitby.

"The Egyptians didn't," said Christopher Rabbit. "Well, the king was beginning to feel a bit worried by now and promised Moses that if the frogs went, he'd let the slaves go. But when the frogs died, the king…"

"… changed his mind again," said Hector.

"That's right," said Christopher Rabbit. "He changed his mind again, so God sent more terrible disasters. There were plagues of insects and flies. Animals died and people became ill. Still the king refused to let the Israelites go.

"Then God sent a great storm and huge hailstones rained down on Egypt, but the king wouldn't give in."

"I'd have given in by now," said Hector.

"So would I," agreed Caravan Bear.

"I don't know that I would," said Runt. "I don't like being bullied, and it seems to me that God was acting like a bully."

"No, he wasn't," said Whitby. "Just think about those poor slaves and the awful lives they had! If we're talking about bullies, I think the king was much worse. I think he was cruel and wicked! He didn't care about the slaves and he didn't care about his own people either."

Christopher Rabbit went on. "Then God sent a plague of locusts, who ate all the crops so there wasn't any food."

"What was Moses doing?" asked Caravan Bear.

"Keeping his head down and keeping quiet – that's what I'd do," said Hector, quietly snuffling at the grass.

"He couldn't do that," said Christopher Rabbit. "He'd promised God. After every disaster, he went to the king and asked him to let the slaves go free. By this time some of the king's advisers were getting worried. 'Please let them go,' they pleaded. The king thought about it and agreed, but then…"

"… changed his mind," said Hector, Whitby, and Caravan Bear.

"So God sent a great darkness over the land that lasted three days. The king was furious. 'Get out of my sight!' he shouted to Moses. 'If you come back, I'll have you killed!'

"Moses told the king that because he wouldn't free the slaves, God would send one last dreadful punishment. At midnight, every first-born son in Egypt would die."

Everyone was silent.

"That's pretty bad," said Whitby.

"Do you think God meant it?" asked Caravan Bear.

"I think God means what he says," said Christopher Rabbit.

"Well, I still think God's a bully," said Runt obstinately.

"Look at it this way," said Christopher Rabbit. "God had made a promise to the Israelites and they trusted him to keep his promise.

"If you were God, who made the world and everything in it, you'd want to care for the people who believed in you and trusted you. You wouldn't want to see them beaten and starved and worked to death. You'd want them to be free to worship and love you. Wouldn't you?"

"Not really," said Runt.

"Just as well you're not God then, isn't it?" murmured Hector.

"And it's not as if God didn't give the king lots of chances to change his mind," Caravan Bear pointed out.

"The king *did* change his mind."

"And kept changing it back again."

"I don't think God wants any of us to be slaves," said Hector slowly. "I think he wants everyone to be free."

"I feel sorry for poor old Moses," said Whitby suddenly. "What an awful job he had going back and forward to the king."

"And his brother," said Caravan Bear. "I mean, he was the one who actually had to speak to the king."

Christopher Rabbit went on with the story. "God gave Moses instructions for the Israelites so that their children would be safe. And at midnight, every first-born son of the Egyptians died."

"Wow," Whitby gasped.

"After this last terrible disaster, the king finally gave in. He told Moses to take the Israelite slaves and leave

Egypt. And that's what they did."

"And that's the end of the story," said Whitby, getting up and shaking sand off her tail.

"No," said Christopher Rabbit. Whitby lay down again.

"God promised the Israelites a land of their own, but he didn't tell them how to get to it. He didn't want them to go by the shorter route as they might meet enemies they'd have to fight. So he led them on a longer route into the desert."

"How did they know the way?" asked Hector.

"God showed them the way. He went in front of them as a column of cloud in the day and a column of fire at night."

"Satnav would have been easier," said Hector.

"It hadn't been invented," said Caravan Bear.

"What did the king do without all his slaves?" Runt suddenly asked.

"That's a good question," said Christopher Rabbit. "What do you think he did?"

"He changed his mind!" shouted Runt triumphantly.

"Yes. He changed his mind. As all his slaves had gone, he had no one left to build his great cities. By this time, of course, he'd forgotten all about the disasters."

"Wasn't much of a king, was he?" said Whitby thoughtfully. "You'd have thought he'd have learnt by now that God was more powerful than him."

"No, he wasn't much of a king," Christopher Rabbit agreed. "He sent his army out into the desert to find the Israelites and bring them back. He thought that as his soldiers went on horseback or in chariots, they'd soon catch up with the slaves who were on foot."

"If I'd been an Egyptian horse, I'd have refused to go," said Hector stubbornly.

"I'm sure you would," said Christopher Rabbit. "The Israelites, who had set up their camp near the Red Sea, saw the army getting closer and were terrified. 'Why did you take us out of Egypt to die here in the desert?' they said to Moses. 'It would have been better for us to have stayed slaves in Egypt!'

"Moses told them not to be frightened. 'God will save us,' he said."

"You mean they were stuck between the sea and the army?" said Whitby. "How scary."

"I wouldn't be scared," said Runt. "I'd have trusted God."

"I thought you didn't like God," said Whitby. "You said God was a bully."

"Maybe, but he was the strongest," Runt replied.

"By this time, the army was almost on top of them," Christopher Rabbit went on. "God told Moses to hold out his staff over the water."

"What's a staff?" asked Hector.

"A kind of stick, I think," said Caravan Bear. "It's what humans sometimes use to help them walk."

"That's because they've only got two legs instead of four," said Runt.

"Moses held out his staff and, with a great whoosh, the sea parted on each side, leaving a clear, dry path straight through. The cloud that God had used to guide the Israelites through the desert moved behind them so that the Egyptians couldn't see what was happening. The Israelites began walking on the path through the sea."

"What about the fish?" Whitby asked suddenly.

"What do you mean?"

"What happened to the fish when the sea parted?"

"I expect they were all right," said Christopher Rabbit. "It doesn't say anything about the fish in the story, but they probably got swept up in the great

walls of water on either side of the path."

"What happened to the Egyptians?" asked Caravan Bear.

"Well, all night long the Israelites walked down the path right through the Red Sea. By morning, they had reached dry land on the other side.

"When the Egyptians could see what was happening, they followed the Israelites onto the path. God told Moses to stretch out his staff again – and the great walls of water came rushing in, and all the Egyptians drowned."

"Wow," said Whitby.

"And that's the end of that part of the story," said Christopher Rabbit, closing the Bible. He looked around.

It was a lovely evening. Far too fine to go inside. Caravan Bear fetched his guitar, sat on the caravan's steps, and began to play.

"I bet *I* can play," said Runt. "Here, give me!" He made a grab for the guitar and broke one of the strings.

"Now look what you've done!" Whitby shouted at him.

"It's all right, I can mend it," said Caravan Bear, bending over the broken string.

"It's not all right, it's all wrong," said Whitby hotly. "He grabs your guitar without asking just when you were going to play for us. He's rude and he's horrible and I wish he'd go away!"

Without another word, Runt got up and began to walk off. Christopher Rabbit and Caravan Bear looked at each other.

"I'll go after him," said Christopher Rabbit.

He caught up with Runt at the edge of the sea.

"Nobody likes me," said Runt. "I don't know why."

"Well," said Christopher Rabbit, "they probably would if you thought a bit more about others and tried to be helpful."

"I don't know how," said Runt. Christopher Rabbit thought he looked very small and very sad standing there at the water's edge.

"Why don't you go back now and say you're sorry?"

"What for?"

"Well, for stowing away. Then for grabbing Caravan Bear's guitar and breaking the string."

"Will that make them like me?" asked Runt.

"It's a start," said Christopher Rabbit.

Runt began walking back over the sand toward the caravan. Christopher Rabbit watched him go, then turned and looked out over the sea.

The sun had just dipped below the horizon and the sky was aflame with red and gold. Shadows lengthened along the beach.

Christopher Rabbit looked back to the caravan. Runt and Whitby had begun to collect twigs to make a fire while Hector, his head in a large bag of oats, snorted contentedly. Caravan Bear, having mended his guitar, was strumming it quietly.

"Thank you, God, for this beautiful place," Christopher Rabbit said. "Thank you for the story and for my lovely friends. Help Runt become a nicer pig – he's not really bad, just a bit thoughtless."

And he made his way back to the warmth and light of the caravan.

9

Ruth's New Home

"Time to go home," thought Caravan Bear, looking anxiously at the repairs he had to do to the caravan. He walked around it. Its bright redness had faded and the yellow wheels were grimy with dust and dirt. He would give it a fresh coat of paint.

"Time to go home," thought Hector the horse, looking forward to a good lie-in in his stable. He had been on the road towing the caravan for a long time and although he had enjoyed it, he would like a rest.

"Time to go home," thought Whitby the dog. Although she had loved all the adventures they had had, it would be good to lie on a rug in front of the fire.

"Time to go home," thought Christopher Rabbit

sadly. He thought of his home, which he had left in such a hurry all those months ago. It would be sad and neglected. He hadn't even washed up, so there would be piles of dirty dishes in the sink. He thought how lonely he would be and heaved a big sigh.

"Time to go home," thought Runt the pig, who had stowed away in the caravan. Runt wasn't sad. In fact, he was looking forward to boasting of his adventures to his brothers and sisters.

They packed their belongings, hitched Hector to the caravan, and set off down the long road that led away from the beach of golden sand and the blue, blue sea.

Their first stop was the farm where Runt lived. As they went in through the farm gate, Runt's brothers and sisters and mother and father came trotting to meet him. Runt climbed down the steps.

"Goodbye, then," said Caravan Bear.

"Goodbye," said Hector and Christopher Rabbit.

"Goodbye," said Whitby, who was very glad to see the last of him.

"Bye," called Runt over his shoulder. "You'll never guess where I've been!" he shouted as he went to meet his family. "I've been to the sea!"

They all trotted off to the pigsties, Runt talking all the time.

"He never even said 'thank you' for feeding and looking after him," said Whitby.

"Did you expect him to?" asked Caravan Bear.

"Not really."

Hector pulled the caravan around and they turned away from the farm.

They carried on for many miles. Caravan Bear, Whitby, and Hector sang as they went and Christopher Rabbit joined in, but he didn't really feel like singing.

They finally parked for the night in a cornfield. The corn had been harvested and all that remained on the ground was stubble. The caravan bumped over the rough ground with Hector complaining that the stubble tickled his legs.

After supper, Caravan Bear looked at Christopher Rabbit.

"Would you read us another story?" he asked. "The last one of this holiday?"

"If you like," said Christopher Rabbit, who didn't really feel like reading anything. He would rather have gone for a long walk so that he could be miserable by himself without upsetting his friends.

He picked up the Bible and looked through the pages.

"How about... the story of Ruth. Would you like that?"

"How do we know if we'd like it?" asked Whitby. "We don't know what it's about."

"We've liked all the other stories Christopher Rabbit has read us, so I'm sure we'll like this one," said Caravan Bear, and he and Whitby settled themselves comfortably inside the caravan. Hector stood outside, his head poking through the window.

"Many, many years ago, a man called Elimelech, his wife, Naomi, and his two sons left the town of Bethlehem and went to live in another country called Moab."

"Were they caravanners like us?" asked Whitby eagerly.

"No. They went because the harvest had been

poor and no one had enough to eat. After a while Elimelech died, but Naomi wasn't left on her own because she had her two sons. The sons married two local girls, but some while later both her sons died."

"Bit of a sad story," said Hector.

"It gets better," said Christopher Rabbit, looking at the end of the story. "Naomi's daughters-in-law…"

"What's that?" asked Hector.

"It means her sons' wives," said Caravan Bear.

"I didn't know that," Hector grumbled. "It's all very complicated with people dying all over the place."

"They didn't die all over the place," Caravan Bear explained carefully. "They died in a country called Moab."

Sometimes, he knew, Hector could be a bit slow in understanding. "And it isn't complicated. First of all Naomi's husband died, then, a long time later, her two sons died, leaving their wives…"

"…who were called Orpah and Ruth," Christopher Rabbit went on. "They were kind girls, and when Naomi decided that she wanted to return to her home in Bethlehem where her family still lived, they said they would go with her."

"Was there enough food by then?" asked Whitby.

"Yes, there was," Christopher Rabbit replied. "So Naomi, Orpah, and Ruth packed up and set off for Bethlehem. But on the way Naomi kissed the girls, gave them a hug, and told them to go back to their own homes and their own families. She probably thanked them for coming so far with her."

"Why didn't she want them to go any further?" asked Caravan Bear.

Christopher Rabbit thought for a moment. "Probably because she thought it wouldn't be fair to take the girls into a strange country where they didn't know anyone. The customs would have been different, perhaps even the language.

"Anyway, the girls didn't want to leave Naomi, but she persuaded them. At least, she persuaded Orpah, who kissed her mother-in-law goodbye and set off back to Moab. But Ruth wouldn't go. 'Don't ask me to leave you,' she said to Naomi. 'Where you go, I'll go, and where you stay, I'll stay. Your friends and your family will be my friends and family, and your God will be my God.'"

"That was kind of her," said Caravan Bear.

"Why didn't she go back to her own home when

Naomi told her to?" asked Hector.

"Perhaps she wanted a change," said Whitby. "Perhaps she wanted some adventures. *We* all wanted to see different things and have some adventures, which is why we've been away in the caravan. Perhaps she wanted the same."

"There's a difference between going away on holiday like us and going away from your home and your friends for good," said Caravan Bear. "I think it was a brave thing to do."

"So why did she do it?" asked Hector again.

"I think it was because she loved Naomi," said Christopher Rabbit. "And perhaps she felt sorry for her because Naomi's husband and two sons had died. She didn't want Naomi to be on her own. Anyway, Naomi and Ruth went on and at last arrived in Bethlehem. The women who lived in the town gave Naomi a big welcome."

"How were they going to live?" asked Caravan Bear.

"Well, they'd arrived in Bethlehem just as the barley was about to be harvested. Ruth decided to go to the fields and follow behind the reapers in order to pick up any bits of barley they dropped. It was

called gleaning. This would give them some food."

"Didn't they have machines to do the harvesting?" asked Hector.

"Not then – they did it all by hand."

"Rather a boring diet," said Whitby, wrinkling her nose. "Barley, more barley, and even more barley. I wouldn't like it."

"You would if that was all there was to eat," said Caravan Bear.

"The owner of the field, a man called Boaz, noticed Ruth when he came to see how the harvest was going. 'Who's that girl over there?' he asked his manager. 'She came back from Moab with Naomi,' said the manager. 'She came here early this morning to ask my permission to pick up any stray bits of barley and she's been working hard ever since.'

"Boaz went over to Ruth. He told her not to work in any other field but his. He said that he would make sure she was safe. He also told her that when she was thirsty, she should go and get a drink from the water jars that the men had filled."

"Why did he do that?" asked Whitby.

"Because he was a kind man. He was also related to Elimelech."

"Who was he?" asked Hector.

"Naomi's husband who'd died, stupid," said Whitby impatiently.

"I'm not stupid. I'm just a little slow at times," said Hector.

"Not when you're towing the caravan," Whitby said with a grin.

"That's different."

"Shall I go on?" asked Christopher Rabbit.

"Yes," said Caravan Bear.

"Ruth asked Boaz why he was being so kind to her."

"Yes, why was he?" asked Whitby.

"Boaz said that he had heard how good she had been to Naomi. He'd heard how she had left her mother and father and home to go with Naomi and live in a foreign land. So he told her to glean as much as she wanted, drink whenever she was thirsty, and also told her that she could eat with the reapers at mealtimes."

"It's a funny thing," Hector said thoughtfully.

"What is?" asked Caravan Bear.

"One kind thing seems to lead to another. If I've been nice and not grumbled when you've wanted to travel further than I wanted, you're usually nice back and give me a good bag of oats to eat. What I mean is," he went on slowly, "that if you're nice to others, they are often nice to you."

"You're not as slow as I thought," said Whitby, impressed.

Hector bowed his head. "Thank you."

"And it works the other way, too. If you're nasty to others, they might well be nasty back," said Caravan Bear.

"Like Runt," said Whitby.

"Oh, he's not nasty," Caravan Bear replied. "He's just young and rather selfish."

"Isn't that the same as being nasty?" asked Whitby.

No one could answer that, so Christopher Rabbit went on with the story. "Boaz also told his people to drop some stalks of barley on purpose so Ruth would have plenty to take home.

"Naomi was very happy when she heard how Ruth had got on. So Ruth went out into the fields each day until the barley and wheat harvests were over. She and Boaz became friends and eventually they married. Naomi was delighted, especially when Ruth and Boaz had a little baby boy. And that's the end of the story."

Christopher Rabbit closed the Bible.

"What is a friend?" asked Whitby suddenly.

"It's someone who looks after you and gives you oats when you're hungry," Hector answered.

"I don't eat oats," said Whitby. "Or barley," she added.

"I think a friend is someone you get on with," said Caravan Bear slowly. "But that's just part of it."

"I think a real friend isn't selfish," said Christopher Rabbit, after some thought. "Ruth might not have wanted to go and live in a different country, but she did because she loved Naomi and didn't want Naomi to have to go on her own."

"Naomi wasn't selfish either," said Whitby. "She could have told the girls they had to come with her, but she didn't."

"I think a friend is someone who keeps their promises," said Caravan Bear.

"I don't always keep my promises," said Whitby. "I can be really bad at times."

Caravan Bear laughed. "Not really," he said. "But you try anyway, and we all make mistakes."

"I think a friend is someone who cares about you," said Christopher Rabbit slowly. "Whatever you do or whatever you say, a real friend always wants the best for you."

"Like God does?" Whitby asked.

"Yes. Like God does."

Everyone was quiet for a while thinking about this.

"You're all good friends of mine," Christopher

Rabbit said at last, feeling very sad. "And I'll miss all of you."

Caravan Bear smiled at him. "We'll miss you too," he said. "But we'll meet soon and have more adventures."

"You really want me?"

"Of course we do."

"We wouldn't think of going without you," said Hector grandly.

A few days later the caravan stopped in the road outside Christopher Rabbit's home and, with a heavy heart, he climbed down the steps – carefully, as he was carrying the Bible.

"Goodbye," said Caravan Bear.

"Goodbye," said Whitby.

"We'll see you soon!" Hector called as he started off up the road.

"Not too fast, Hector!" said Caravan Bear, hanging tightly on to the door. "You'll overturn the caravan!"

"Nonsense!" snorted Hector and gathered speed. Christopher Rabbit watched them go up the road and disappear in a cloud of dust.

"I'll miss you," he said quietly. He turned, took a deep breath, walked down the path, opened his front door, and stopped in amazement.

"Happy homecoming!"

Christopher Rabbit blinked. The room was full of his neighbours, who were standing, lying, and perching around a table that groaned under a weight of food.

He looked around. His home was bright and shining. It was clean and highly polished. There were no dirty dishes in the sink.

"What…" stuttered Christopher Rabbit, "…how…?"

"We knew you were coming," said Min, trying to balance a glass on her tail, "so we thought we'd welcome you home."

Min the cat lived next door to Christopher Rabbit. She prided herself on knowing everything that was going on.

"It was Min's idea," said Henry the beaver. "She saw you go off in that caravan-thing and then told us when you'd be home."

"How did you know when I'd come home?"

"It was a little pig somewhere or other," Min explained, looking very pleased with herself. "A sparrow who was flying over the farm at the time

heard this pig telling everyone about the adventures he'd had with some animals in a red caravan with yellow wheels. The pig mentioned something about a rabbit who told stories. I guessed it was you.

"Well, the sparrow passed the news on – you know what birds are like for gossiping," she added disapprovingly. Min wasn't fond of birds. "And at last the news reached us."

"Then I saw you on the road when I was out collecting nuts, and ran over to say you'd be here today," said Susie the squirrel.

"But that's so kind of you all," said Christopher Rabbit, quite overwhelmed.

Henry coughed in an embarrassed way. "Think nothing of it," he said.

"You left in such a hurry that you hadn't locked your door," Min went on. "I thought it would be a pity if you came back to a dirty home, so I told the others and we decided to clean it for you. When we started, we found these…"

She waved her tail to a pile of invitation cards in the middle of the table.

"… you hadn't delivered them…"

"… which was why we didn't know about your

birthday party..." said Maurice the mole.

"... which was why we didn't come..." added Henry.

"So this is a kind of late birthday party and welcome-home party all rolled into one," Min ended triumphantly.

Christopher Rabbit sat down suddenly.

"I don't deserve friends like you," he said.

"Nonsense," said Henry. "Have a drink. Have something to eat."

It was late by the time everyone had left. Min stayed to help clear up, and when she had gone, Christopher Rabbit sat down in his favourite chair in front of the fire, a glass of elderflower in his hand.

"What a stupid rabbit I've been," he thought. "It was all my fault that no one came to my party."

He thought some more.

"But if I *had* delivered the invitations then I wouldn't have met Caravan Bear, Whitby, and Hector and wouldn't have had so many exciting adventures. And I wouldn't have found the present of the Bible."

He took a sip of his drink. "Did you leave it for

me, God?"

He finished his drink, stretched, and stared into the dying fire.

"I'm not sorry it turned out as it did. I'd never have made such good new friends or found out how good all my neighbours are. And I'd never have learned that there are so many wonderful stories in the Bible. Thank you, God, for everything that has happened and for all my kind friends, old and new. Help me to be a good friend in return."

And he went to bed.

The story continues in...

The Animals' Caravan

Stories Jesus Told

1

A Cold Start

"Close the door!" said Hector the horse angrily as Caravan Bear opened his stable door, letting in a wave of cold air.

"It's not that bad," said Caravan Bear.

"Yes, it is," said Hector. "I wouldn't mind if it were winter, but it's supposed to be spring."

"It is spring – and time we were off on our travels!"

Every spring Caravan Bear would hitch Hector up to the caravan and, with Whitby the dog, they would set off in search of new adventures. Every autumn they would return to the paddock and the small patch of garden where they would stay until it was spring again.

"You go, then. I'm staying here in my nice warm stable."

Caravan Bear went up to Hector and stroked his nose. "Now, what is all this?" he asked. "You love going away."

"Yes, but not when it's cold and wet. Anyway, you said you had work to do on the caravan."

"I've done it. Well, most of it."

"Why can't we go in a week or two when the weather's better?"

"You know we can't. Christopher Rabbit is expecting us."

"Can't he wait?"

"It's his birthday."

Whitby ran in, her tail waving behind her.

"Come on, Hector – time we were off!"

Hector began nibbling some hay.

"He doesn't want to go," Caravan Bear explained.

"Yet. I want to go but not yet," Hector retorted. "I'll go when it's warmer."

"We can't let Christopher Rabbit down," Whitby cried. "It's...

"... his birthday," Hector finished. "I know. What's so important about Christopher Rabbit's birthday?"

"It's when we first met him. Don't you remember? He was standing in the road, holding this big book in his hand, and..."

"...and I nearly ran him down, silly animal."

"But then he came with us on our travels and read us those wonderful stories from the Bible."

"And we had a lovely summer," Caravan Bear went on. "You said it had been the best summer you'd ever had."

"All those adventures..." Whitby added.

"Yes, like getting stuck in the rain," Hector grumbled, not wanting to be convinced.

"Oh, don't be such a misery," said Whitby.

"Well, we can't let Christopher Rabbit down, so we're going just as soon as I've finished a few jobs and packed the caravan," said Caravan Bear. "And I'd better go now or we'll be late." He smiled at Hector. "If it's cold, you can wear your warm new coat – the one we gave you for Christmas. Very smart you'll look, too!"

With that, Caravan Bear and Whitby left the stable.

"Shut that door!" Hector called after them, but he wasn't really angry. He was remembering how much fun they all had last year. He was also thinking how good he would look in his new coat.

"Where are we going first?" asked Whitby,

prancing around Caravan Bear as they went over to the caravan. It was standing looking very fine in its bright new coat of red paint and its brilliant yellow wheels.

"Here, there, wherever the fancy takes us," said Caravan Bear – as he always did at the start of their adventures.

He looked proudly at his handiwork and smiled happily.

*****

Christopher Rabbit looked anxiously out of the window; then, for the tenth time, went over to the door, opened it, looked up and down the street, sniffed the air, and closed the door again. Would they come or wouldn't they? They had said they would come on his birthday and today was his birthday, but he hadn't heard anything from them – and the weather wasn't really ideal for starting out on holiday. It was grey and cold and beginning to rain.

All day long there had been a procession of his friends from the village, wishing him a happy birthday, bringing him presents, hoping he would have a good trip, and asking him when he would be going.

"Soon," he had said. "I'll be off soon." But as the day wore on, he became less sure.

His small bag that he had packed two days before sat forlornly by the front door. On top of it was the Bible.

Now that had been a strange thing, Christopher Rabbit remembered.

It was on his birthday last year that he had run out of his house, upset because no one had come to his birthday party and no one had given him any presents or cards. He smiled as he remembered that no one had come because he had forgotten to post any invitations. But at the time he thought he didn't have any friends at all. So he had put on his scarf, rushed out of the house and fallen over a brightly wrapped parcel that had been left in the road outside his front gate. The handwritten label said CHRISTOPHER RABBIT in large letters.

Inside was a book. A big book with the words THE BIBLE on the cover. When he opened it, he found the handwritten words "Read Me" on the first page just inside.

Then a caravan had come hurtling down the road toward him. He had been sure he would be run over.

But the caravan stopped just in time and Caravan Bear, Whitby, and Hector had invited him in. A spring and summer of wonderful adventures had followed.

He had been very sad to leave them and go home at the end of the holiday. He thought the winter would be very long and very lonely without his new friends. But it hadn't. Surrounded by friendly neighbours, the time had soon passed.

He had helped Henry the beaver and his family when the dam they built across their stream overflowed and their home had been flooded; he had dug the dormouse out of a snowdrift; he had searched for fresh nuts when Susie the squirrel's hoard had been stolen; and in the evenings he would often find Min, the cat who lived next door, curled up on his hearthrug in front of a warm fire. In fact, he had been so busy he had not even had time to open his Bible, let alone read the stories inside.

Perhaps he would have time now, he thought, once they were all off on their travels.

If they were off on their travels.